This book is given to:

_____

Date: _____

From:

_____

Check out some of my favorite stories:

_____

_____

_____

_____

_____

_____

_____

WORDS DO MATTER

Ping-Pong, Parkinson's, and Parables

The power of words in a collection of original
stories and sayings

KEVIN PACE

Dedication

I met someone in January 2002 who encouraged me to cultivate and write down my thoughts. She inspired me tremendously. Her faith and conviction helped me make a connection with my spiritual side. For the encouragement and insight she gave me throughout this endeavor, I am dedicating this collection to my beautiful bride, Marla Pace. Many of these stories are drawn from simple acts and everyday occurrences. These are the inspirations for my writing. Marla has lived many of these events. She has the heart of a champion and the compassion of an angel. Thank you, Marla, for all that you do.

Contents

Introduction

As one of ten national finalists in Oprah Winfrey's Nissan "Quest for Inspiration," Kevin and Marla Pace have made quite an impact with their Words Do Matter ministry. Their amazing collection of original images and original sayings has captivated the hearts of people throughout the world. They produce ready-to-frame original prints of Marla's pictures and Kevin's words.

They call it "God's sense of humor," and it has transformed a corporate numbers-geek and a stay-at-home-mom into a husband-and-wife team that is inspiring the world. Their story of facing and overcoming adversity is a living testament to how God can turn burdens into blessings.

Chapter 1: Revelation (Our Story)

Revelation: Announcement, disclosure, surprising fact, enlightenment, heightened awareness, calling.

"And you shall know the truth, and the truth shall make you free" (John 8:32).

What to consider:

- How do you deal with change-, good and bad?
- What causes one to persevere despite dramatic challenges?
- How do you maintain a positive attitude despite setbacks?
- How are you using your words to be a powerful force?

Chapter Foreword by Kevin Pace

I thought I had success all figured out. Why didn't everyone do it? I breezed through school. I worked full time through college, possibly setting the Indiana University record for Bs. I paid my own way through college—no financial aid and no debt. I learned just how hard I had to work. I got married and started a family (three kids, a dog, and two cats). I began my career at Bloomington Hospital as an accountant and quickly moved up to management. I bought a big house (went into debt) and nice cars. I started going to church early on and was saved as a teenager. I learned all the Christian words to speak. I had worked my way to success. I…, I…, I…, I. I had learned to play the game. God had a different plan, a much different plan.

The *Pain* Inside the *Pane*

At age 41, I found myself alone for a week in a sleep-eight, use-it-or-lose-it Tennessee condo. There I was, staring outside at the beauty of a magnificent ice storm. The weather was squelching any hopes for a mind-renewing week of golf. The shimmering brilliance clinging to the trees wasn't the only storm raging that day. The storm within, the pain inside the windowpane, the attack of body against mind was challenging everything I knew and threatening my very existence. It was a mutiny of motion, a collapse of communication, and a rebellion of spirit. I knew the storm outside would pass. The storm inside was a different story.

At age 33, I had watched my doctor noticeably struggle to deliver a Parkinson's diagnosis. God was issuing a wake-up call. I, however, had decided I was much too busy for such an inconvenience. Instead I hit the snooze-button—several times. After eight more years of running on the hamster wheel I had created, Parkinson's had slowly and silently robbed me of almost everything. Gone were my family, my finances, my faith, and my hope.

When you stand in the presence of remarkable storms, A remarkable presence of character forms.

For many years, Parkinson's was just a nuisance, an inconvenience of circumstance causing me to change certain behaviors. I managed to hide it from most people—those not really paying attention anyway. At work, I found myself hiding away in my office, scheduling meetings over the phone rather than in person. Over time, the burden of a 24/7 constant reminder that something is terribly wrong can be devastating. Parkinson's is relentless in its attack, insidious in its approach, and far-reaching in its wake. It attacks its victims physically, mentally, socially, and spiritually. It had slowly and methodically stolen everything I had worked for.

In anguish I cried out, "Dear God, what do You want from me?" In complete frustration, I typed on my laptop, "What if *God* is just a hoax?" Staring at the screen, my eyes fixated on the words. It was as if they just blended together in a white fuzzy ball. As I refocused, I replaced the words with, "God, use me in whatever way You need to serve Your purpose. I am willing." It was a tearful, fearful, life-changing moment. Though I had been a Christian since childhood, it was my first true act of faith. It was my first time being vulnerable and admitting that I couldn't do something myself. After years of being a casual Christian, I decided to listen to God instead of telling Him what I was going to do. Finally, I had decided:

THE MOURNING IS OVER

A twitch of my finger that didn't feel right.
A prelude to battles I'm destined to fight.
A message my body was attempting to give.
Stop speeding through life and learn how to live.

Life passes you by when you go way too fast.
Things that take time are things that will last.
The voice grew stronger and louder each day.
I'd speak to my hand, but it wouldn't obey.

This inner rebellion, this fight for control,
A breakdown of mind, of body, and soul.
My thoughts were, Ignore this ridiculous stand,
When my foot then decided to join with my hand.

What once worked together as a unified team,
Defiantly mocked the pursuit of my dream.
A spiritual turmoil, a conflict had dawned:
My body's left side, reluctant to respond.

I went to the doctor to confirm what I felt.
A Parkinson's diagnosis was unjustly dealt.
A woe-is-me attitude came out for a while.
A guilty conviction without going to trial.

I started to withdraw so others wouldn't see,
The insidious destruction going on inside me.
We all have our struggles or demons we face.
I've learned to live life at a much slower pace.

But the mourning is over! I now am confessing,
This burden I bear is more of a blessing.
I don't fly through life like I did once before.
Enjoying the journey, you see so much more.

What I used to condemn, I now, "Thank God!"
I refuse to be shaken by Satan's façade.
God gave me a purpose, it's my humble prayer,
This might be a blessing to someone somewhere.

I grabbed my Bible and it fell open to Judges, where I read the story of Gideon. Gideon's story is quite intriguing. He too was a bit of a loner. Frustrated, Gideon lamented his challenges, fixating on the burdens of his people. His country was being ravaged by a massive army of gypsies and thieves who repeatedly stole their harvest and burned their fields. In the midst of Gideon's anguish, an angel appeared, claiming, "Hail mighty man of valor, God is with you!" You would think Gideon would have been surprised or fearful at the angel's appearance, but his response seemed almost apathetic. The first thing that struck me about this interaction was how God had instructed the angel to address Gideon. Such high expectations for someone the world saw as the least in his tribe, which was the least of the tribes in his country. When you look in the mirror, you might see a nobody, but God sees a champion and a mighty warrior. God sees not only what you've done, but what you will do. I also liked Gideon's response. I can almost see him rolling his eyes, "Yeah, right, God is with us? Ha. If God were with us, why must we suffer from disease, hunger, and pain? Why, if God is on our side, are we tortured, beaten, and left for dead? What good is it for God to be on our side?"

When courage checks out and bravery flees,
Rise to the challenge by bending your knees.

Why don't we give out our heartfelt applause
To our Father who loves us despite all our flaws?

Ah, Gideon had asked the question for the ages, "Why does God allow terrible things to happen?" What I liked was God's non-answer. The angel responded to Gideon, "Go in your power and save your country." God says, "You don't like the way things are? Go change it! You have the power, the strength, and the authority to do so." Consistently throughout the Bible, God does not answer whines or complaints; He simply says, "Change your circumstances." Gideon, despite his reluctant response to the angel, took the challenge and, without even raising a sword, defeated one of the largest armies in biblical history.

MAN OF VALOR

Their country had suffered for so very long.
An enemy army stood one million strong.
They came every year. There were no reprieves
From cave dwelling drifters, gypsies, and thieves.

They traversed the desert like pirates on sand.
When harvest would come, they'd ravage the land.
Like spiders in a web, devouring their prey,
Consuming whatever would stand in their way.

Death and destruction would litter their wake,
But that wasn't all they had managed to break.
The hopes of a nation, extinguished by fears;
Autumn was coming, the battleground nears.

Gideon was part of the lower class tribes,
And least among them, as the Bible describes.
He did his own thing and no one could see,
The champion inside him that one day would be.

Then an angel appeared from out of the blue,
Saying, "Hail man of valor. God is with you!"
Gideon looked around as if he'd not heard.
"What did you say? That's completely absurd.

If God were with us…" Gideon extolled,
"Then why must we suffer? I have to be told.
Why are we tortured with death and disease?
Answer me that and I'll bow to my knees."

The angel responded, ignoring his plea.
"You have the power to go set them free!"
For God won't respond to complaints about *Why?*
His answer? "Go change it," demanding they try.

"But, I'm just a shepherd? What could I do?"
The angel said, "God sees a warrior in you."
So Gideon accepted God's challenge to fight.
People would follow as he stood for what's right.

He placed a few men in the enemy's way.
He fooled the great army into running away:
Oppression defeated without raising a sword.
A victory of faith, a blessing from the Lord.

Hunger? Go feed them! Sick? Find the cure!
God gave us the ability to make it occur.
No matter what troubles we find ourselves in,
Like Gideon, God gives us the courage to win.

When the challenge of life has filled up your cup,
Listen for angels to shout out, "Rise up!"
You are the one who can open closed doors.
Go, save your country. The power is yours.

I got the message. It was a conscious decision to turn my burdens into blessings. Ironically, outside everything was frozen in place, unable to break free from its captor; while inside everything I had held captive for forty-one years was melting away. "Okay, God, I am Yours—now what?" As I stared at my blank screen, it was much like my life—nothing to show. Suddenly, I was uncomfortable with the emptiness. Suddenly, I became consumed with the thought of filling the empty space. Suddenly, my fingers began filling the screen with words. I typed, "In the beginning…"

for it felt like mine. I opened my Bible to Genesis. I noticed something I had never noticed before. It didn't read, "God created the world." It became obvious to me *how* God created the world. "God *said* let the earth take form" (and so forth). I thought to myself, why would God speak the words? Why would the author not just say, "Then God created"?

Life can become so abundantly clear, In the midst of a storm that heightens our fear.

Who was He talking to? God had created us by speaking us into existence with His words. Then He said we were created in His image. I had to ask myself, "What have I been creating with my words?" The answer to that question was confusion, anxiety, suffering, and pain. The words of the angel came quickly back to mind, "Go in your power, and change it." I typed, "Grandma was wrong: *Words Do Matter.*"

The reason it seems I struggle with stress, Is directly the result of words I confess.

Before I knew it a story was unfolding before my eyes. It was as if I was alone in a theatre, watching the premier of a movie with the task of recording whatever I saw. I had to keep typing to see what would happen next. By the next morning it was done—a novel entitled *A Test of Faith*. For an accountant who had never written anything more than a few interoffice memos, it was a "God-inspired" experience. God had given me new hope and a new dream.

Another odd thing happened that week. In need of a break, I ventured out to a local ice cream shop. Sitting in the corner enjoying a shake, I remembered a shop my mom and I frequented. This particular shop carried a unique flavor called *licorice voodoo ice cream* made from black licorice. No one could believe I really liked it, especially my mom. For some reason, I thought maybe I could write about it. Maybe I could write a commercial or a marketing campaign. Out came a napkin; out came a pen. As the words in my head began cascading through my fingers, the oddest thing happened—the words began to rhyme.

LICORICE VOODOO

The ice cream sign read, "Unique Sensation!"
A tantalizing twist in a strange combination.
What were they thinking creating that dish?
An eerie concoction of black licorice.

It sounded like such an intriguing new taste:
Vanilla cream mixed with black swirling paste.
Soon after devouring my delectable cone,
I flashed a big smile, and the damage was shown.

The customers cringed at the horrible sight,
As if I were haunting their Halloween night.
I looked in the mirror at the dark hefty toll:
Inside of my mouth was now black as coal.

It looked pretty bad, I couldn't deny,
As if I were poisoned by black liquid dye.
I often consider why that flavor didn't last,
Why it dropped from the list so incredibly fast.

Perhaps all the screams or outspoken cries,
Perhaps from the laughter in onlookers' eyes.
But, likely it was, when the workday was done,
They counted the sales, which totaled just one.

Should it ever return, that flavor so fine,
You know I'll be back to be first-one-in-line.
Until then I'm satisfied simply to dream,
Of that flavor called licorice voodoo ice cream.

Chapter 1: Revelation (Our Story)

Poetry, I thought, *I hate poetry.* What few poems I had read made little impact on me. I thought they were boring, unmarketable, and mostly didn't make any sense. Why would I be writing poetry? *Go figure,* said the accountant in me. But secretly I had to admit—it was kind of fun and addictive. It was like a big word game, a puzzle that had to be configured just right. My numbers-oriented mind liked the symmetry and the exactness of how a poem was constructed. The stories started coming, one after another.

If you call me a poet, I won't disagree,
But inside I'll cringe, 'cause I know that's not me.

At first I thought, *What was God thinking?* Why would He provide such an unlikely talent? I just didn't get it. I was so hung up on how God might use me, I forgot to consider why. After much deliberation, the light finally began to shine. What better way for God to get His message out than one contrary to the way everyone thinks? If He delivered His message through polished proven professionals with perfected deliveries, it would likely come across as a marketing pitch. It is the message that is important, not the delivery and certainly not the messenger. Who more unlikely to write inspirational poetry than a seasoned, self-proclaimed numbers-geek? Who more unlikely to deliver a message than someone embarrassed to speak publicly because his body begins shaking from his disease? I do have to admit, it is not really something you would brag about, being the least likely to succeed at something. Thanks God, I really needed that revelation. What God did know, which may be more of a character flaw than a talent, was that I am a big dreamer, entirely too stubborn to quit, and that I would never complain (well, maybe a little).

I did try to remind God that rhyming poetry is viewed as amateurish and childish, often discouraged by the literary community. Most publishers won't even consider poetry because they would be deluged with submissions. Finally I decided, who am I to argue with God? If He says to wear black socks with my shorts, despite what others may think, I'm going to do it.

The mountain before you will move from your way,
If you *tell* it to move and *believe* what you say.

Confirmations came quickly when I met Marla, who would become my encourager, my best friend, and my bride. She is a battle-scarred warrior with an incredible story. Her servant's heart and her tested faith gave me the courage to follow God's calling. In early childhood, a rare hereditary brain disorder called arterial vascular malformations (AVMs) flared up— blood clots in the brain. She woke up one morning with eyes crossed and weakness on her right side. This stroke-like attack would set her back but not keep her down. At sixteen she met her first love. At eighteen they were married and started a family. She was living the American dream, but carrying a time bomb inside of her. The stress of delivering her first child caused her second brain episode. More physical setbacks, but her determination outweighed any discouragement. Two years later her doctor told her not to get pregnant again; it would kill her. She already knew the seed of life was within her. Despite strong advice that she abort her unborn child, with a self-defense rationale she refused. As she went under anesthesia for a C-section, she said her good-byes knowing she'd likely not come back. She is a tremendous fighter.

When the forces of evil parade on your soul,
You carry the power to take back control.

Having fought through the battles her body was causing, a third, this time major, brain reaction occurred. Doctors gave her little hope that a rare major surgery dangerously close to her brain stem would work, but it was all they knew to do. They said they "lost her" five times during that eighteen-hour brain surgery, which resulted in some drastic medical measures—a major facial nerve, a balance nerve, and a hearing nerve had to be cut. She woke up to the good news: "You're alive. However, you probably won't walk again, you've lost hearing on one side, and we think we can fix your face" (which had fallen in on one side). While some would

24

have drowned in their sorrows or rightfully complained about how unfair life was, Marla strengthened her faith and made the decision to glorify God. One week later, to everyone's amazement, she walked out of rehab. Hope had returned. She was a fighter. Then, as if she had not endured enough, eight years later her loving husband, who had courageously stuck by her through all those trials, was stricken with cancer. Marla's caregiver heart quickly took over, but he would lose his battle four months later. A thirty-two-year-old widowed mother of two, battle-weary and battle-scarred, had little reason to praise God, but that's exactly where she put her trust.

A warrior will never entertain retreat; It is never an option to consider defeat.

It was Christmas Eve, 2001. A bright moon filled the sky. Two lonely hearts prayed the same prayer and cried the same tears. One month later, in a series of inexplicable circumstances, I met my beautiful bride-to-be online. Yes, we are a living testament that it really does work. A host of e-mails in our first week established our deep-seated friendship. We decided to meet, even though we had never once discussed or shared what each other looked like. We just knew that a strong bond of friendship would always last. I knew from the moment I looked in her eyes. Marla wasn't quite as convinced. It seemed we were destined to be together. It wasn't the smoothest courtship with so many issues to overcome, but nine months later we said "I do" in front of family and friends (and God).

In 2004, we took a St. Valentine's-week trip to Sedona, Arizona, which not only opened our eyes to the magnificent beauty God had surrounded us with but also to a vision of sharing hope with the world. Marla had always wanted to be a photographer, and I had this creative spirit that was being unleashed more every day. The purchase of a simple digital camera changed our lives forever. When I put captions on a few of Marla's pictures, some friends got excited about it. With the uncertainty of health threatening our financial future, we had been looking for ways to supplement our income. The vision became clear. The next few months were filled with images, words, and graphic design. At my full-time job, however, the stress level was reaching unbearable proportions. My body was not responding well. The door was closing on a twenty-three-year accounting career. As scary as that step was, we knew God was calling us to greater things. My last day of work marked our first day in business for ourselves. The American dream was ours to embrace. We had cast our hopes, pinned our wishes, gambled our future on a few simple words from an inexperienced writer and a few simple images from an unestablished photographer. What were we thinking?

If no one is mocking or laughing at all, It could likely be your dream is too small.

We thought our new business, *Words Do Matter,* might be a way to fund the publication of the stories I had been writing. We quickly discovered it could be much more than that. God had so many others more qualified to choose from, but He knew one thing—we were willing. Our first step was to do a small art and craft show. For $100, we decided to contract a ten-by-ten vendor booth at the Riley Festival in Greenfield, Indiana. Having no vendor experience whatsoever, we made multiple mistakes. We did, however, see the mission field opportunity. We were hooked.

Then a businessman we respected advised us to do the Indianapolis Home Show. It was truly a test of faith, as we invested $3,000 into a booth with no guarantees of any sales. The centerpiece of the show is a huge showcase home built inside the building. Vendors fight for years to get the best spots. We got in the show just a few days before, relegating us to an unwanted spot, tucked in behind the house. God knew what He was doing. When they went to build the house, it wouldn't fit, and they had to turn it just a bit. This last minute parting-of-the-sea led us right to the exit of the home tour. Hallelujah! I can't say we made lots of money that week, but we covered our expenses and caught the thrill of sharing the work God had entrusted to us. One lady was walking briskly past our booth, when she suddenly stopped and came in. She said the Holy Spirit had drawn her in. That was all the confirmation we needed.

Since 2005, we have been sharing our work with crowds at art and craft shows. Throughout the 150-plus shows we have done, the common reaction is a look of amazement, followed by, "We've never seen anything like this before." Marla, a true prayer warrior, blankets the Holy Spirit over our booth wherever we go. At one point, we even received recognition from Oprah Winfrey. She was holding a "Quest for Inspiration" contest, seeking those utilizing their talent to inspire the world. We filled out an information sheet, pointed them to our website, and were selected as one of ten national finalists.

When you choose to chance unlikely dreams, You change the way unlikely seems.

I would love to tell you everything worked great and we rode off into the sunset living happily ever after. That is not the case. God still had a refining work to do in us. After all, Satan now had something to lose. Before the business, he had us right where he wanted—not doing anything. We had taken a major pay decrease by leaving my career. With pharmacy prescriptions totaling almost as much as our mortgage each month, we desperately searched for ways to make our business work financially. Then, a benefits insurance company literally stole over $100,000 in benefits due us. We spent years in a legal battle over benefits with no real resolution (although the lawyers all made out pretty well). We went through things that would break most couples up or would at least deter them from their dream. For us, it made us stronger. We learned how to live below our means. We learned how to tithe when we had no idea where we were getting our next meal. We learned how to lean on each other, and our love grew even stronger. By faith, we survived those challenges. Most of our friends didn't even know we had struggles because we didn't share. We knew from the beginning that God would keep His promises.

When you glorify God through trials you face,
Your faith will empower the gift of His grace.
Then when the world stands up to applaud,
You'll know where it's from and give it to God.

It was the Indianapolis Home Show 2009. We were struggling to make ends meet, so the last thing we thought we needed was a major ice storm, leaving the show virtually vacant for four of the ten days. It just so happened the show promoters were putting on a big show a month later at Lucas Oil Stadium. Being bored by the lack of guests at the show, I casually asked our representative if we could set up a ping-pong table. Table tennis has always been a passion of mine.

That simple conversation would lead us down a remarkable path. Because the promoter had a connection with ping-pong and Parkinson's, he donated a $10,000 space for a "Ping-Pong for Parkinson's" promotion. We had a month to prepare.

With help from the owners of the Table Tennis Club of Indianapolis (my regular hangout), we quickly put a list together of competitors willing to showcase their skills. The challenge was, we needed a not-for-profit organization to accept donations. Surfing the web, I found a newly formed organization called the Indiana Parkinson Foundation. It was started by the children of a fellow Parkinson's sufferer. It is a remarkable story. Check it out on their website: www. indianaparkinsonfoundation.org. They had formed an exercise class called "The Climb," which greatly improves the lives of people with Parkinson's. We fell in love with their story, their resolve, their family, and their outwardly spiritual commitment. We have been so blessed by all the members and participants over the years. The event was a huge success.

The reason it seems opportunity's door
Swings open to those who don't need any more,
Is because they've prepared themselves in advance
For precisely the moment they are given a chance.

It was two weeks later when a local news anchor called. Anne apologized for being out of town for the event, but explained she heard about it and had checked out our website. She said she wanted to do a story about us and our work. We were blown away. Anne spent three days with us. The first day, she came alone, sat on our living room floor, and we just talked. She was very gracious as we shared our story and she shared part of hers. We were impressed by her generous spirit. She completed the story a couple of months later. God intervened again. The story was scheduled to air in May but got bumped twice for breaking news. The day it aired was the day before I went in for a Deep Brain Stimulation (DBS) surgery to help relieve some of my Parkinson's symptoms. The timing could not have been more perfect. We felt like celebrities as the nurses made a fuss over the story. We can't thank Anne and her team enough for what they have done for us. We don't really feel like we did anything. We just reacted to our circumstances. The video can be found on our website on www.wordsdomatter.com.

Today, Words Do Matter has gone wholesale in addition to doing art and craft shows. We are selling to retailers who do the selling for us. We don't get the same customer interaction, but retailers are sharing our story with others. It is all in God's hands. The world is a place where evil can methodically and strategically break down biblical values. Words Do Matter is using those same techniques to honor God, raise awareness, inspire hope, and connect purpose-driven people throughout the world. Jesus said, "Go and make disciples." So be it.

Opportunity shines in the depths of despair,
At times we are spent, with nothing to spare.

Marla and I live close to Indianapolis, Indiana. Though we have our physical struggles, we have been blessed immensely. We have five awesome children (three are married as of now) along with five (and hopefully more), adorable grandchildren. They all live within an hour of us, which is a tremendous blessing.

I used to wonder why God wouldn't heal me; then I considered that maybe Parkinson's was my healing. I often think, where would I be without it? I certainly wouldn't have the personal relationship I have with Christ. I would probably be stuck in a high-rise office, working on a spreadsheet. No one really appreciates or rarely even understands a creative interactive spreadsheet. However, you can write encouraging words that inspire them, and they will be amazed. We love our life and the journey God has given us.

Parkinson's and brain surgeries have taught us to slow down (literally). We now enjoy life, basking in the beauty of God's creation. If you are following your calling (and you do have one), God bless you. If you aren't sure, then go find it. We've often questioned, who are we to think we could make a difference in this world? Thank goodness that two thousand years ago eleven scared men, huddled in a room, given the task of sharing the gospel, did not think that way. You are a child of God. You have a mighty and magnificent purpose. Are you too busy to find it? Are you negotiating the deal? Are you ready for the peace that comes from embracing the thing you were meant to do? Remember the words of Gideon's angel, "Hail mighty man of valor, God is with you. Go, in your power and save your country."

It occurred to me God wasn't likely to say,
"It never occurred, I should do it your way."

"Why's it so hard?" you're tempted to ask.
"Does it have to be such a difficult task?"
When you finally win, you'll know it's because
No one wants to hear, "How-easy-it-was."

The thing about life we're unable to see
Is where we are going and who we will be.
At times we may crack, at times we may bend,
But God sees our life from beginning to end.

All that you need, if you want to succeed,
Is found in a book, if you simply will read.

If I were a fish, I'd tell all my friends,
That worms come on hooks with sharp, pointy ends.

Chapter 2: Love

Love: Joy, happiness, affection, comfort, romance,
security.

"You shall love the Lord your God with all your
heart, with all your soul, and with all your strength"
(Deuteronomy 6:5).

What to consider:

- The blessings of loving and being loved.
- How can you build your loved ones up with your words?
- How do the words you speak affect the love that you show?
- Do you show your love for God in your words to Him?

Derek and Stephanie Evelo are very successful realtors in the Indianapolis, Indiana area. They call their impressive sales staff the Evelo Team. The thing that impressed us most about Stephanie and Derek is that they are always on the same page. They complete each other. They are raising three great boys in a Christ-centered home. The romance they show in their everyday lives has made an impression on many, including us. The way they complement each other is something very special. Their willingness to give without any expectations is remarkable.

Make a Difference. Change Lives. Leave a Legacy.

www.EveloTeam.com

Guest Foreword by Derek and Stephanie Evelo

We first met Kevin and Marla at the Indianapolis Home Show. We were intrigued by their artwork and their outward Christian beliefs. You don't often see people boldly display their beliefs in public, yet the outward display of their values matched our inner conviction and our own beliefs. That made for an instant friendship. Their approach was simply to share, not sell. We created an incredible bond with this couple. So, when they asked us to help sell their home in Greenfield, Indiana it was a perfect connection. Kevin and Marla, through their struggles, have exemplified the Christian walk. They do everything together, and their relationship has prospered because of it. We *love* what they are doing in sharing what God has given them.

Love is a word that is often overused. We love this, and we love that. We feel it's not a word to be taken lightly. This is why we were very careful before we shared those three simple words, *I love you,* with each other in our relationship. *Love* is a word that we strive to put value on in raising our three boys. We use love and relationships as the cornerstone to our family and our business. In real estate, disagreements often arise. We strive to handle each situation with the love of Christ. God is love. Can you imagine that God loved us so much that He sent His only Son to die for us so that we may live forever with Him in heaven? It's unfathomable that someone could love us *that* much, yet God is love. It's that simple. He loves us—unconditionally, always, and forever.

—Derek and Stephanie Evelo

REMARKABLE STYLE

A sweet Southern belle with an eloquent poise,
Upholding the hope that tradition enjoys.
A charm that exudes like a soft woven quilt.
An element of grace very carefully built.

A calm guiding hand, always soft and serene.
With exquisite class, so exact and pristine.
She carries a strength, a compassion of heart.
She's bold with conviction where others depart.

It's not handed down through family lines.
Her title is earned. Her character defines.
For something unsought, she adorns it so well.
This magnificent beauty, a true Southern belle.

REFLECTIONS

Time has a way of reflecting the past,
A beautiful portrait of memories cast.
A few years ago, when you said you would,
I thought that I loved you as much as I could.
But now looking back, the reflection is clear,
My love for you grows with each passing year.
You are my light when darkness entails.
You are my hope that always prevails.
You are the sunshine that warms me inside.
You are my love, my beautiful bride.

GET OUT OF THOSE SHOES

If you could step out of those shoes for a day,
And look on yourself in a different way.
You might have a totally new point of view,
Discovering things you don't know about you.

If you could step out of those shoes for a while,
And witness the way you make people smile,
You'd be quite amazed at what we all see.
You'd let those inadequate feelings go free.

If you could step out of those shoes to relax,
You would see in yourself how an angel reacts.
You might understand how you make people feel.
You'd no longer harbor fears you conceal.

If you could step out of those shoes and reflect,
It would bring such a wondrous healing effect.
The magic you carry would finally show,
The incredible person you don't seem to know.

I wrote these next lines for Marla on our first anniversary. Unfortunately, I may have set the bar too high.

"I've made a few choices I've come to regret.
I've done a few things that I'd like to forget.
The two best decisions I've made in my life,
Christ as my *Savior*, and *you* as my wife."

A MYSTERY TO ME

I know when her eyebrow goes up a degree,
Something is up, that we must disagree.
I won't have a clue what it could be about,
A mystery, of sorts, I must now figure out.

When she claims, "Nothing's wrong," in a stoic reply,
Something is wrong and I better know why.
Likely it's something she thinks that I thought,
Something perceived that really was not.

I could take the "innocent of everything" stand,
But it's not likely true, I do understand.
Regardless of fault, regardless of blame,
I must recognize, there are rules to this game.

The first rule is, there is no chance to win.
Attempting to do so will be treated like sin.
The second rule follows, if trying to guess,
Sarcasm won't make the pain any less.

Rule number three—any blanket attempt
To apologize will only be met with contempt.
A deadly mistake is rule number four,
Claiming you'll, "Not do whatever anymore."

The last rule is this: don't try to defend,
Or try to make light to make it all end.
The best thing to do is accept you were wrong,
And hope that it all goes away before long.

GOOD MORNING, SUNSHINE!

I woke her up early, a quarter past five.
"It's a beautiful day, let's go take a drive."
She didn't jump up and exclaim I was right.
Instead, "Go away, it's the middle of the night."

"C'mon," I said, "trust me. Let's go and explore."
I knew of a place she had not seen before.
I finally convinced her to get up and go;
I promised her one unforgettable show.

I drove her that morning to a place that I knew,
With a panoramic scene from a mountaintop view.
Below in the valley as far as could see,
A misty cloud winding like roots of a tree.

The lights from the city like stars all aligned:
A painting so perfect, God's blessing defined.
Then a bright glowing ball on the horizon arose,
Rays of light danced with a brilliant repose.

Breathtaking, beautiful, awesome, serene.
No words could describe what I had just seen.
A moment like that, I could never replace.
It wasn't the sun, but the look on her face.

Though she won't admit it, this happened exactly like this in Branson, Missouri in 2004. It was a gorgeous morning. We have shared many more since then.

JUST TELL HER SHE CAN'T

Don't tell her she can't, whatever you do,
Or that is the path that she will pursue.
Her eyebrow will raise, ideas will spin.
It won't be too long before she must begin.

Something inside her will seek to disprove,
The notion that anything, "Simply won't move."
At times it is handy. At times it is fun.
She'll tackle whatever they say, "Can't be done."

The effort involved is not her concern.
At times I will watch, if only to learn.
She's always consistent, I've studied her style.
Challenge her ways, and she'll practice denial.

Experience reveals the way she'll react.
I've used it before, as a matter of fact.
I told her, "No way, you can't possibly be,
In love with a wannabe poet like me."

Marla and I share a storybook kind of love. I'm the accountant; most would consider me to be the organized one. I don't hold a candle to her. We lovingly tease her because she alphabetizes her spices. She is the most caring person I have ever met. I am the idea-guy, hurling idea after idea. She is the get-it-done type. In many ways we are completely opposites, but we get each other.

Marla truly is a throwback to ages past. She is an admirer of traditions and a builder of legacies. She is truly *a character with character*. My brother-in-law, J.C., was so tickled by her that he started calling her "Old School." It fit perfectly.

OLD SCHOOL

She's set in her ways. We call her, "Old School."
The older the better is her golden rule.
No gizmos or gadgets or new-fangled toys.
Hi-tech electronics, she says, just make noise.

She mashes potatoes and bakes her own bread.
Her grandma's old quilts adorn the sleigh bed.
Instilling traditions she makes the kids keep;
Convictions are strong for beliefs that run deep.

A heritage upheld and a legacy created.
An evening at home she calls underrated.
She's carving out memories we'll always recall.
She loves all the colors of leaves in the fall.

Antiques are her passion, she loves shooting stars.
From her point of view, horses trump cars.
She puts all her trust and faith in the Lord.
She lives life below levels she can afford.

She seeks to please God, her one simple goal,
Concerned by the things that reach to her soul.
With the heart of an angel, she's never been cruel,
My beautiful bride—just call her "Old School."

I was the kind of kid who was always a little unsure of himself. I had glasses by the second grade. Because I loved sports, I was always breaking them, which lead to having tape on the edges. Mom was a farm girl, not really into the dress-for-success thing. She pretty much let me wear what I wanted. I still remember my favorite pair of wide, pink plaid bell-bottom pants (as my sisters laugh). Most people would say I was shy. I don't think that's true, but I'm not one to be the center of attention. I was, however, especially shy around girls. Here's one interaction my friends talked me into:

THE FIRST YES

It was Halloween night nineteen-seventy-four.
My hope stood behind a formidable door.
I was fourteen years old, not quite a man,
Beginning to question my ridiculous plan.

With palms full of sweat, my bony knees shook.
My friends were all hiding as I turned back to look.
"You can do it!" one said, pointing to the bell.
I raised up my finger, not feeling so well.

What was I thinking, accepting this dare?
I wished I could be anywhere but right there.
My heart began pounding, my stomach, a knot.
I was chilling and shaking, despite being hot.

I couldn't back down, I'd been far too bold,
Terrified at what the next moment might hold.
The door then swung open before I could hide.
Trick-or-treaters came out from somewhere inside.

Suddenly I faced what I had most feared.
My body stood frozen it must have appeared.
My mouth felt as if it were stuffed full of cotton.
The reason I'm here? I must have forgotten.

Then the most beautiful sight I had seen,
Sarcastically grinned and asked, "Halloween?"
"Uh, no," I stammered, dropping my head,
Staring at the top of my shoes now instead.

Hands in my pockets, I was squirming around,
Having lost the ability to muster a sound.
She stepped on the porch and turned the light on.
"Would you like some candy before it's all gone?"

"Okay, I mean no; it makes me break out."
Oh my gosh! What on earth am I talking about?
She asked, "Would you like to sit on the stools,
Pass out some treats to the goblins and ghouls?"

I nodded as my fear became tempered and tamed.
"I think that I like you," I abruptly exclaimed.
For one shining moment my life was complete,
As she uttered the words that sounded so sweet.

"I think you're nice, and I like you too."
Words that still echo my mind like brand-new.
We passed out some treats and sat for a while.
When I asked her out, she said "Yes" with a smile.

When she closed the door and went back inside,
I couldn't just sweep my emotions aside.
Turning, I pumped my fists toward the sky.
My vertical jump must have been three feet high.

A couple of friends were still waiting for me.
"She said yes!" I shouted, "Were you able to see?"
I could have been walking around among kings,
A warm fuzzy feeling that memory still brings.

Not much ever came of that Halloween romance.
I remember one movie, maybe one dance.
For that first big crush from a scared little lad.
What a magical impact that first *yes* had.

RENDEZVOUS

It was a long day at work so I stopped at a bar,
Unwinding a bit at the Old Shooting Star.
I'd never done anything quite like this before.
I'm pretty laid back, just a homebody bore.

She looked out of place, I tried not to stare.
Do I take a big chance? I don't know, do I dare?
Sitting on her right, some big wrestler guy.
I came in from the left and simply said, "Hi."

I saw the dude gave me a back-off glare.
But, she was so gorgeous, I just didn't care.
I said, "Hey there, darling, can I buy you a beer?
I don't think I've ever seen you 'round here."

"That's your best line?" she sarcastically said.
Slick, who agreed, started shaking his head.
I answered, "No, ma'am, no lines if ya please.
I'm just an ole country boy, likes what he sees."

Smiling, she questioned, "A hillbilly line?"
Mr. Stud started flashing the big loser sign.
So, I said, "Pretty lady, let's be totally up front.
We know why we're here, we know what we want.

I think you and I should hook up somewhere."
She then looked away like I wasn't even there.
Laughing so hard, Mr. Cool spilled his drink.
Both of us wondering, just what did she think?

She turned back and said, "That sounds mighty fine.
At least you were honest. Your place or mine?"
I threw down a twenty and extended my arm.
She grabbed it with style and sweet country charm.

Looking over my shoulder, back through the door,
Mr. America was picking his jaw off the floor.
We stepped on outside, with a kiss on her cheek,
I said, "Honey, where did you find such a geek?"

"I thought he was cute," she said, just to tease.
"But I do feel sorry for the next girl he sees.
I'll pick up the kids, and meet you at home,
Or should I say, 'back where the buffalo roam'?"

Leaving, I shouted, "Hey girl, by the way,
I fall more in love with you every single day."
She smiled and replied, "I did like your line,
But if you ever forget, Mr. Macho is mine."

There was one girl in high school who brought out the best in me. She was a part of the church youth group. I can't say I ever had romantic feelings for her, but I loved being around her. She was so much fun, and funny in an off-the-wall sort of way. She was one of the popular kids but never acted that way. Had we not met in youth group, we would have never been friends. She saw me as a project. She was bound and determined to transform me. She changed my hair, convinced me to get contacts, and encouraged me to dress differently (so differently). In turn, I helped her with homework and gave her a shoulder to cry on when someone treated her badly. She married a good friend of mine who later became a very fine pastor. I don't know what went wrong, but when the military called them overseas, something happened that I will never understand. Anorexia is a horrible and greatly misunderstood disease. The story happened this way almost word for word:

TO MANDY JO

In honor of Amanda Jo Abel (Carnegie)

She called me her friend. She was one of the few.
She saw in me things that no one else knew.

I was backward and shy, a chess club bore.
I had tape on my glasses. Need I say more?
She was one of the popular kids at school.
But she crossed the line, broke an unwritten rule.

Intrigued by her interest, seduced by her smile,
She freshened my outlook and polished my style.
She taught me to soar like an eagle would fly.
I gave her a shoulder when she needed to cry.

We promised that no matter where life would lead,
We'd always **come running** if ever in need.
She married a friend and moved far away.
Her homesick heart was begging to stay.

With nowhere to turn and no friends to find,
She created a place to escape in her mind.
With an inner-rebellion that raged deep inside,
She barely resembled that beautiful bride.

Her body was ravaged—a self-induced crime.
She'd withered away in such a short time.
She looked in the mirror and actually said,
"I'm so overweight. I wish I were dead."

Prophetic words from the shell of a soul
Who engaged in a battle and lost all control.
She tried to convince us that she had been cured,
Unaware of the damage her heart had endured.

As I ran down the hall to the emergency door,
A shake of his head said, "She's with us no more."
Anguish screamed out at this undeserved fate.
My promise was broken. I'd shown up too late.

I wanted to tell her but I was too scared.
I'd practiced the words that never were shared.
Why didn't she stop? Why couldn't she see?
Why didn't I help her like she had helped me?

I saw in her things that no one else knew.
She called me her friend, but it wasn't true.

Chapter 3: Motivation

Motivation: Urgency, desire, passion, purpose, reason, drive.

"Delight yourself also in the Lord, and He shall give you the desires of your heart" (Psalms 37:4).

What to consider:

- How do your words help in your desire to excel?
- How has someone's words encouraged or motivated you?
- How does speaking positive words affect your attitude?

Jordan Hulls is our nephew. In 2009, he was named Indiana's Mr. Basketball, leading his high school team to an undefeated season. He went on to be a standout player for Indiana University 2009-2013 and is currently playing out his dreams overseas. He won the hearts of fans everywhere with his intense desire to win. If you met him, you would immediately see his humble Christlikeness. On the court he has a team-first mentality. Off the court, he is always thinking of serving others first. He was thrown into rock star status because of his ability to throw a ball through a hoop. How he has handled that with grace and dignity is nothing short of miraculous. Jordan has discovered how important motivation and preparedness is on the basketball floor and in raising his God-focused family.

Jordan runs a skills camp each summer for area youth, called JH1 Skills Academy. He and his family founded the Never Lose Hoop Foundation to help kids affected by cancer. As a testament to his character, Jordan signs every autograph with a reference to Philippians 4:13.

Guest Foreword by Jordan Hulls

When I think of how amazing God's plan is for each of us, my Uncle Kevin and Aunt Marla instantly come to mind. Their story is incredible and there's no denying the role that God played in it. Just as God has given me basketball to use as a platform, He has given them a special platform of words to inspire, support, encourage, and motivate others to serve Him.

Motivation is something that has never been an issue for me. Basketball has provided me with a very unique platform. I am blessed to be able to share not only my basketball experience but also the huge impact Christ has had on me throughout my life. "Dreaming big" and "working hard" were the sayings that helped me accomplish my goals. I try to encourage kids to do the same with whatever they're passionate about. God has put me in a position in which I can use my basketball platform in order to impact others. I can't thank Him enough. This is my fourth year playing in Europe in four different countries—Poland, Kosovo, Belgium, and now Germany. During my career, I've learned many life lessons from different cultures. Two things that I've learned while going through difficult times: 1) Have faith in God's plan and 2) use the talent God has given you. People always told me that I wasn't big enough, fast enough, strong enough, or just flat out good enough to play basketball at a higher level. That doubt motivated me. With the unrelenting support of my family and close friends, I was able to use my faith in God's plan and motivation to end up where I am today. It's a great feeling—being able to prove people wrong and achieve the goals you set for yourself. However, knowing it was part of God's plan all along is an even greater feeling. He motivates me every day to become the man He wants me to be.

—Jordan Hulls (Philippians 4:13)

COMPETE

We stick out our necks, exposing our chins.
We compete face to face to determine who wins.
Though many don't like the methods we choose,
If we recognize **victors**, someone must lose.
But the best way to fail is not to compete,
It's losing that makes our victories sweet.

Back in my younger days (wow, that sounded really old), I played and coached a lot of softball. I took pride in teaching people how to hit. Though never a power hitter, I could usually manage to line one up the middle. I would simply wait for my pitch, visualize, and take the same swing every time. Consistency is a key in any sport you play. What I found was that most of the people I taught were more influenced by what the rest of the team was doing rather than their task at hand. If the team was hitting, they were hitting. If the team was in a slump, they were in a slump. Hitting is contagious. Teams get *hot*, and for the moment are unbeatable. Find someone who can change the team momentum, and you have a true leader. Find someone who can *hit* when no one else is, and you have a powerful force. What about finding someone in a church who can totally change the momentum? What if you find someone who is so on fire for Christ, they become contagious to all? How much momentum could your team have? How valuable would that be to the community? What would that kind of fire do to your congregation? What if that fire was in you?

BILLY THE KID

Billy was twelve when we met on the field,
Determined to discount a past he concealed:
His third straight year on a nine-year-old team;
They allowed him to play because this was his dream.

The other kids teased him for being so small.
It's not always height that makes someone tall.
He bounced on the grass with a confident strut.
Something was wrong, but I didn't know what.

"Hey, rookie!" he shouted, and began to approach.
"I'm Billy the Kid, the assistant coach."
With hat turned around and eyes focused in,
"If you'll listen to me, I'll teach you to win.

We still need a shortstop, if you've got the game.
I guess we'll find out. Have you got a name?"
"Rookie will do," I smartly replied.
"I'll play what position the coaches decide."

He gave me a smile, then proceeded to say,
"I'm getting called up to the big leagues someday."
It was just about then he got hit on the head.
A baseball that, oh, "must have curved," so he said.

He jumped to his feet. I was laughing inside.
His love of the game could not be denied.
A friendship developed from unlikely souls.
Our differences great, but we shared the same goals.

Together we dreamed and worked on our game.
His effort relentless, and always the same.
I've never seen anyone work quite so much.
His mind disbelieving any physical crutch.

A positive outlook and fresh point of view:
He actually believed his dream would come true.
"It's a matter of heart," he often would say.
He taught me to fight, I taught him to play.

He'd speak of the day that we'd answer the call.
"Imagine," he dreamed, "major league ball."
On the crest of our hopes, Billy became sick.
His overworked heart was going down quick.

50

Tears filled my eyes as I raced to his side.
Consoling me, Billy said, "What a great ride!"
"Imagine," he whispered, "I'm getting the nod,
Lead-off hitter on God's All-Star Squad."

I said, "You deserve all the blessings you'll get.
Just watch out for curves, and try not to get hit."
With his eyes focused in, he said, "It's the end.
Thank you for being my very best friend.

I just have to tell you, before I must leave,
My dream will live on in what you achieve.
You've got the talent, I know what's inside.
Don't ever give up," he said as he died.

He gave me the dream he cherished the most,
The only thing left for which he could boast.
Now standing on deck, my first big league shot.
If only Billy… was my wishful thought.

"Hey rookie!" I heard, "Check out the board."
A message that Billy took time to record.
"Congratulations," he said, "on your rookie debut.
I've taught you to win, it's now up to you."

I homered that night, on the first ball pitched,
For battles he fought and lives he enriched.
I'm humbled by what all the sportswriters did,
They changed my name, William, to "Billy the Kid."

Billy is about a thirteen-year-old kid who played on my son's nine-year-old team. He was small from spending several years of his young life in the hospital. What stood out about this kid was his unwavering positive attitude. Despite his challenges, he was like a beacon of hope.

FEAR-AVOIDERS

When the thing we must do, we don't do for fear,
The thing we must do becomes painfully clear.
When the fear of not doing the thing we must do,
Becomes greater than the fear of following through,
Then the thing we must do, we'll no longer delay,
And we'll wonder what it was that we feared anyway.

THE BATTLE

Sometimes it's the battle we don't want to fight,
The one we put off or place out of sight,
The one we ignore so it might fade away,
The dragon we don't think we're able to slay,
The thing that if only we took time to do,
Could bring out the champion residing in you.

Even when no one else thinks you can win,
Claim it out loud before you begin.

What resides in the heart of a champion is found,
In what they will do when there's no one around.

Don't ever lose Hoop!

52

The Cubs finally did it. I always said I would have to pull this story should they ever win! Nah!

A CUBS FAN'S LAMENT

A storm of depression, an emotional frost;
The series is over, Chicago has lost.
We never had much to cheer for before,
Losing was something we chose to ignore.

By now we're accustomed to coming in last,
A heritage transcended from many years past.
But, this year we knocked upon victory's gate,
Attempting to change what many call *fate*.

We discovered that *almost winning* is worse
Than just simply losing and blaming the curse.
The glimmer of hope this season shone bright,
Casting some doubt that we'd lose every night.

In Cubby tradition, let's go make some trades,
So this hope of contention eventually fades.
Then, when we lose, it won't matter at all.
It's safe on the bottom, with no place to fall.

The mystique of a Cubs fan, a humble appeal,
A love for the game that no one can steal.
Before we'd have cheered that the season was done;
Now we're lamenting, "If only they'd won."

A coach of mine had the guts to teach me this lesson. He wasn't much on celebrating. His favorite saying was, "Act like you've done it before."

RESPECT IS EARNED

There once was a time I thought I was good;
I could make any play a great player could.
If I failed to get something I thought that I should,
I'd get angry and mad like a competitor would.

My body would contort, my head would roll back
In attempts to admonish the skill I must lack.
I called it intensity, my competitive side,
Where confidence and arrogance sometimes collide.

Then one day a coach, who had earned my respect,
Asked me a question that I didn't expect.
It was after a grounder that barely got by,
Left me shaking my head and questioning why.

He quietly sat down on the bench next to me,
Then spit on the ground, and patted my knee.
He said, "Son, you can play, you're one of my best.
But be careful the way you stand out from the rest."

I questioned, "Coach, I don't know what you mean."
He said, "Don't be a spectacle, creating a scene.
Are you trying to convince them, by slamming your fist,
That you should have made the play you just missed?"

He then made his point deliberately slow,
"'Cause it ain't really workin' I want you to know.
If you want to impress them, that stuff won't do,
Just go make the play, then act like you knew."

"Respect will be earned by keeping your cool,
Not acting like some kind of wannabe fool.
The way you react is the thing they'll recall,
So show a little class in the way you play ball."

THE LAST ONE PICKED

My palms would sweat. I'd feel physically sick.
Why was I always the last one they'd pick?
There were times I would not be selected at all,
For a physical game, I was pretty darn small.

I watched as they'd point, whisper, and scheme,
Avoid, if they could, choosing me for their team.
My dad told me, "Son, God made you this small,
To prove it's not height that makes someone tall."

He set up a goal post, bought me a tee.
He told me success was determined by me.
So I worked on kicking whenever I could.
I practiced at times that no one else would.

They still picked me last, for nobody knew,
What in my backyard I had learned how to do.
Who could forget those hot summer days?
High school tryouts to determine who plays.

The teasing began when I stepped on the field,
My helmet so big that my eyes were concealed.
The coach even grinned, and chuckled out loud,
"We should have explained, no children allowed."

I stuck out my chin, looked square in his eye,
And said, "I'll show you, Coach, just give me a try."
The practice was brutal, much more than I thought.
But then, toward the end, at last came my shot.

Coach asked who would like to be kicker this year.
As hands all flew high, the team gathered near.
He explained how important a kicker would be,
Last season they had lost four games under three.

He placed the ball down on the thirty-yard line,
Forty-yards from the goal I had claimed to be mine.
Whoever came closest was whom coach would pick,
To carry the honor and responsibility to kick.

There must have been twenty or more who had tried,
All woefully short as the coach loudly sighed.
With hands on his forehead he looked to the sky.
I was the last to step up and ask, "Can I try?"

Everyone laughed 'til he shouted, "Enough!"
Then mockingly said to me, "Show us your stuff."
As I carefully positioned the ball on the tee,
It seemed the whole world was now laughing at me.

So, I called on the power that God will provide,
Then glanced to a nod from my dad on the side.
Three big steps later my toe struck the ball.
I caught it just right. I knew how, after all.

It seemed like slow motion, the team stopped to stare.
The ball gently tumbled as if floating on air.
The looks on their faces I could never replace,
As it split through the uprights with plenty of space.

I looked toward my dad, now beaming with pride,
Then turned to the coach with his mouth open wide.
Cheers were replacing the laughs I had feared.
Despite any struggle, my dream persevered.

I went on to college and professional ball,
But that was the kick I enjoyed most of all.
I don't think I'd ever have worked quite that hard,
If I wasn't picked last on that old schoolyard.

Mom and Dad were great supporters of mine. "The Last One Picked" was my dad's favorite. It began with the first line, then the rhyme dictated each successive line. It was more like I was reading it than writing it. I had no idea where it was going or where it would end up.

A HOOSIER TRADITION

The crowd on their feet as the clock ticks away.
No one has left on this tournament day.
With four seconds left, the team is down one.
With the ball in his hand, the countdown's begun.

A glance in the eyes of his opponent to say,
"You can't stop me now, there's simply no way."
One dribble, he stops, pressing toes the floor.
His mind in the zone, determined to score.

From all the hard work, his moment is now.
The shot in the air beats the buzzer somehow.
The ball gently spins, slow motion it seems.
The gym starts to echo of past winning teams.

It reaches the goal bouncing soft on the rim.
Then caroms the backboard and back down again.
It hangs on the iron, slowly rolling around,
Then it gently drops off and falls to the ground.

A gasp from the fans as heads start to fall.
But wait, he was fouled, there is hope after all!
He steps to the line and swishes a pair.
The team hoists him up to cheers everywhere.

That's the way that it goes in a ten-year-old's head.
His hope—one day wearing that jersey of red.
To dream about winning the championship game.
Scenarios change, but the ending's the same.

THE FINAL FORE

In the past, when I asked how well he had played,
His answer was full of excuses he made.
He should've had this, he could've had that,
As if there were some evil force to combat.

He missed a few putts, had some bad breaks,
He hit one just barely outside of the stakes.
He gave all the reasons his scorecard should read
A low enough score to have been in the lead.

As if he were judged on the score he turned in,
He justified somehow a way he could win.
But this time was different as he recapped his game,
He didn't recite all the things he could blame.

He gave me his score, and proceeded to say,
"I didn't play as well as I wanted to play.
I made some bad choices that cost me a few,
But next time I'll know just what I should do."

His game had improved, but now I could tell,
He was mentally ready to do just as well.
I patted his shoulder, gave him a wink,
"That is the way a champion should think."

Golf is a great game to play with your kids. What better way to get four hours one on one with your teenager? The game teaches them so many lessons in life. I wish I could still play, but my balance is off when I swing. I can still ride along though.

IF ONLY

It's often the feat that ***almost*** got done.
The thing that ***if only*** we may well have won.
Could've and should've, maybe and might.
The one that ***if only*** things would've gone right.
Imagine the outcome, were that not to be.
The one surely causing sweet triumph to flee.
The seduction of victory turned into dismay.
The one we remember that just got away.

THE RACE IS NOT OVER

The television crews have recorded their features.
Alone with my thoughts, I sit on the bleachers.
The parties have started, the tallies begun.
The fans have departed. The race has been run.

The winners moved on, just a typical day.
Their victory sweet, but I wish they would stay.
They must think it's over, this marathon race,
But the very best part is about to take place.

I'm not as impressed by those who run swift,
As with struggling heroes, embracing their gift.
Unheralded champions are crossing the line.
Ones the word ***courage*** was meant to define.

As I watch them compete, tears start to flow;
These are the stories that few people know.
An eighty-year old thrusting his arms to the sky.
An athlete on crutches breaks down to cry.

An autistic girl yells, "I made it, Dad!"
A blind man with vision like I've never had.
A boy with one leg being helped by his brother.
A challenged young family, holding on to each other.

A young woman, honoring her husband who died.
A handicapped man who would not be denied.
Each difficult step toward reaching their goal.
A chance at a dream where they're in control.

No trophies or plaques, no interview request.
No pretense of winning, just doing their best.
They won't make the six o'clock broadcast tonight.
Their victory was merely to stand up and fight.

I wrote "The Race Is Not Over" sitting on the bleachers at the finish line of the Indianapolis mini-marathon. My then fiancée, Marla, had raised a lot of money for cancer, honoring her late husband. This was her second year of participating in the fifteen-mile race. Despite her physical challenges, she used her courage and faith to cross the finish line. She brought tears to my eyes. I knew I had found a warrior, a mighty woman of valor. There were many champions who crossed the line that day with very little applause, but that's not what they were looking for. I stood and cheered nonetheless.

ALL CHOKED UP

I remember teaching my six-year-old son, Kyle, how to hit a baseball. He kept swinging under the ball, which makes sense now (he became a pretty good golfer). When I told him to "choke-up" on the bat, he looked at me kind of funny, and proceeded to hold the bat to his mouth and coughed.

MOTIVATIONAL SAYINGS

Willpower comes when you seek to instill
The belief into others of the power of will.

At the end of our rope, the knots that we've tied
From battles we've fought, mistakes we have tried,
Will provide us a way to keep hanging around,
Until the way out of this hole can be found.

You've silenced all those who mocked and made fun,
By doing what they said "could never be done."

Speak of your goals as if they were done.
Claim the victory before you have won.

Most would assume the best way to go,
Is steady and straight, consistent and slow.
But champions look for a way they can soar:
Something that no one has attempted before.

Some of the better lessons we'll learn,
Come as we're patiently waiting our turn.

If you're willing to try more than people expect,
Even if you fail, you will earn their respect.

If you continue to let your discouragement show,
What everyone sees is that *you* need to grow.

It's not that a leader has chosen to lead,
But rather, a choice they have made to succeed.

Leadership comes when you're willing to leave
All that you know to chase what you believe.

No matter how strong, no matter how tough,
The *desire to win* is just never enough.
The ones who will win, when given their chance,
Are those who *desire to prepare* in advance.

If you want to find out who your leader will be,
Watch at the end of a game and you'll see.
With the clock clicking down, the light starts to shine
On who wants the ball with the game on the line.

The best way to fail is not to compete;
It's losing that makes our victories sweet.

The perfect arc, the perfect line,
The perfect sound as leather meets twine.

Champions focus their minds in a way,
They see the result before making the play.

Deceptively small is the difference you'll find,
Between those who will lead and those left behind.

We often are told to avoid all the pain,
But it strengthens our victories, measures our gain.

It's a confidence, courage, and bravery pill.
If you want to succeed, believe that you will.

The thing that you see, before in your mind,
Is likely the result in the end that you find.

Are you ready to race? Are you ready to run?
Have you patiently waited for the sound of the gun?
It's time to get going, it's time to begin.
If you never get started, you never will win.

Competitors prepare for the game to begin,
Champions prepare for a way they can win.

No matter what field, no matter what game,
The steps to success are always the same.

Victories begin to erode if you stay
Lost in the things that you did yesterday.
Keep moving on if you want to succeed.
Others will follow if you choose to lead.

If you look upon every formidable foe
As a chance to advance, opportunity to grow.
If you take on the challenge, determined to win,
You'll have already won before you begin.

You can climb to the top of a mighty oak tree,
Or just sit on an acorn and then wait to see.

If you step to the plate consumed by your doubt,
Or you don't even swing for fear you'll strike out,
You'll never discover the thing that you need.
You must learn to fail before you succeed.

In the depths of despair is where champions rise,
The point when they face what seems certain demise.

If a bit of a push is all that you need,
You now have permission to go and succeed.

As a leader sometimes you blaze your own trail.
The decision is already made not to fail.

The view from the bench is not very good,
When you know you can play, believe that you should.
But, if that becomes your only concern,
There's probably something you still need to learn.

Rarely is skill what sets you apart.
More often than not, it's a matter of heart.

People will respect a champion more,
If it's more than just what they do on the floor.

The size of your dream can always be told
By the size of the problems you allow to take hold.

No matter how old your goal has become,
At least you still have one; that's better than some.

When that which you want becomes what you need,
You'll discover how easy it is to succeed.

So often the boundaries that keep us defined
Are simply illusions we've drawn in our mind.

Chapter 4: Passion (Ping-Pong)

Passion: Motivation, desire, undeniable, conviction, purpose, honor.

"Death and life are in the power of the tongue, and those who love it will eat its fruit" (Proverbs 18:21).

What to consider:

- What are you passionate about?
- Does it show in your calendar?
- How do your words produce passion in your life? In others?
- Passion is an attitude that people can easily see. How do you show yours?

Joe Shumaker has become one of my closest and dearest friends. He has a heart of gold. His way of making everyone feel welcome is rarely rivaled. Joe has taught many the game of table tennis and inspired many to be better people because of his attitude. He is obviously passionate about building people up and creating community. He's also a prayer warrior, which shows in how he serves others. Joe has and will participate in the Senior Olympics (he's that good).

Guest Foreword by Joe Shumaker

I met Kevin when he came into the table tennis club. He was a very good ping-pong player but had a lot to learn about table tennis. His passion for the game was obvious, and he learned quickly. You tend to learn a lot about people by playing a simple game with them (even without talking). We struck up a friendship because I could tell he was a believer. We believers tend to stick together! The friendship grew and blossomed outside the club to include our spouses.

I have utmost respect for Kevin and Marla. We have traveled the world together, and their passion always shines through. I have a passion for encouraging people. It is so cool to watch someone react to an act of kindness when it catches them off guard. It's as simple as a genuine compliment, a door held open, or an encouraging word. People can see how you react to them. Whether you are run by a love of life or selfishness is shown by your actions toward others, your compassion is on display. Jesus was kind and compassionate; that drew people in. He was also passionate about His convictions; that kept them around. Your passion shows in how strongly you will stand for what you believe. Your compassion shows in how you treat others. Jesus set the example. If we want a fulfilled life, full of passion, we must love others and serve others first.

Paul was the most passionate person of biblical times. His belief showed to extremes. He was Jesus' stiffest opponent in the beginning and staunchest believer once he understood. Paul's passion is evident when he said, "Yet indeed I also count all things loss for the excellence of the knowledge of Christ Jesus my Lord" (Philippians 3:8).

—Joe Shumaker

TABLE TENNIS: IT'S NOT JUST PING-PONG!

Arrogantly, I thought I was pretty darn good. What more could I possibly have to learn? The game consists of a paddle, a net, a table, and a little white ball. It seems like such a simple game. It is not. I had played since I was a kid. I could beat everyone I knew. As a somewhat backward kid, I managed to come in second in my high school table tennis tournament. I actually caused the all-everything star athlete to get so mad that he broke his paddle in half with his bare hands. I have to credit one of my friends for helping me improve. Starting out, he really wasn't very good. I used to tell him, "You just love to lose." The opposite was true. One summer we played every day. Starting out, he would get five or six points (in a twenty-one-point match). In the end, he would get five or six points. However, by the end of the summer, he could beat everyone else we knew. We both had improved.

Later that year, in freshman gym class, we had a student teacher. He was a tremendous athlete. He was also arrogant and cocky. Table tennis was "his game." He reviewed all the rules in Barney Fife-like fashion, carefully explaining this was not ping-pong. He began volleying with the best athletes, looking for some competition. After his quick evaluation of their skill level, he boldly declared, "I have a challenge. Beat me, and I will run your laps (a daily ritual) for the rest of the time I'm here. Lose and you run double laps until I'm gone." Everyone looked around, eyebrows raised. Silence. "Anyone? Anyone just love to lose?" That's when my buddy's hand flew up. "Ah, someone with courage," the teacher said. As the challenge ensued, I watched as the teacher quickly found his weaknesses and exploited them. My buddy managed to get about twelve points. The teacher smirked a cocky grin. "Anyone else?" Just then my friend bumped me forward. I hated running with a passion. The teacher looked at me with a condescending grin. "Sounds like your buddy needs someone to run with." After a long, drawn-out glare, I said, "Okay, I'll play." My buddy handed me the paddle, intentionally putting it in my left hand. As the warm-ups began, I could tell he was looking for my weaknesses. I saw the puzzled look on his face when I moved the paddle to my right hand. He managed to get sixteen points, and surprisingly handled his defeat rather graciously, possibly because the regular teacher had shown up and was getting a pretty good kick out of seeing Goliath fall, so to speak.

ON THE OTHER HAND

I opened the door to my table tennis room.
His eyes lit up like a flower in bloom.
He said, "That's my game," with a confident air.
"Do you play?" he asked with a challenging glare.

"A little," I declared, "I'm not all that good."
"Let's play," he responded by slapping the wood.
"I've never been beaten," he wanted me to know.
"Whenever you're ready," I nodded, "let's go!"

A back and forth banter of smashes and kills,
Corners, and edges, and other such thrills.
I was just a few points from victory's door,
When I dropped a few shots to tighten the score.

He hit some white lines and went into the lead.
"Remember," he lectured, "don't ever concede."
When he finally won, he looked so darn proud.
"Victory is mine!" he shouted out loud.

"You're good," I conceded, "I like how you play."
"Keep working," he told me, "maybe someday…"
As they readied to leave, the mistake that he made,
Was telling my wife how well he had played.

"So you won?" she asked. "That's pretty good news.
I've one thing to ask you: Which hand did he use?"
His arrogant smile wasn't there anymore,
As she gave me high fives while closing the door.

One day, I was driving by a place I had driven by hundreds of times. There it was—a sign reading "Table Tennis Club of Indiana." I had to go in and see for myself. The club was packed. The owners were very friendly and invited me to play, but I wasn't prepared. They told me about a session for seniors held two mornings a week. I am a morning person, my wife is not. I thought that would be perfect. Now forty-eight years old, my body had been beaten down by Parkinson's. For periods of time, medicine could help my body perform fairly normally. Without any meds, my body would slow to an almost standstill. Every movement becomes a negotiation between mind and body. Things people never think about, like taking a step, become a challenge. When the Parkinson's medicine turns on, it happens like a light switch. Suddenly, I can move fairly normally. Later they turn off like a dimmer. The challenge is taking medicine at the right point on the dimmer to keep the light on. Too much or too soon, and your body starts dancing around like a nervous salesman with too much caffeine. I was unsure how my body would respond.

Later that week, I ventured into the club, paddle in hand. Though I thought I knew a lot about the game, I would soon be corrected. Joe was the man in charge. He was very friendly and very good at interacting with others. He quickly got me involved. I saw the look on his face when I showed him my paddle—a five-dollar special from a ping-pong set of four. Who knew? Joe starting hitting with me. It was as if I had never played before. When he hit the ball, it was like something magical exploded. When it would hit my paddle, it jumped away with so much power that it was just sailing away. I could feel him adjusting his game down to my level; I knew what that felt like. Then he got a curious look, and asked me how I held my paddle. As I showed him my grip, he looked at me like I was swinging a baseball bat cross-handed.

The thing they'll remember when everything's done
Is the way that you played, regardless who won.

As I played different people, I quickly discovered I was in completely over my head, and it had nothing to do with my disease. When that revelation occurs, a choice must be made. I could just let it die, having lost the illusion that I could really play, or I could see what might happen if I tried. I went time after time. I got beat over and over, but was determined to improve. I still remember the first game I won. I was terribly excited, but I kept my cool to not let them know. As the weeks ensued, I started returning shots I couldn't before and attempting shots I didn't dare try earlier. I made many friends. Joe had a way of creating a community. He gave nicknames to certain players based on the way they played. Mine became *the Wall*, for my unusual knack of returning slams. I've been beaten by eighty-year-olds, eight-year-olds, and everything in between. For me, it is about freedom. Sometimes when I'm playing, I actually forget for the moment about having Parkinson's. That is truly a blessing.

WORTHLESS or PRICELESS?

It was the best cherry cola that I ever had.
It's the aftertaste now that's incredibly bad.
It was 1953, at the corner five-and-dime.
I still think it might have been some sort of crime.

I had saved enough money from mowing some yards,
To buy one more pack of Topps baseball cards.
As I peeled back the wrapper, anticipation grew.
My hope to discover an all-star or two.

But treasure doesn't always appear like one thinks.
"Nothing!" I shouted, "This totally stinks."
Some rookie named Mantle was all that I found.
What were the chances that he'd stick around?

My buddy there with me, a big Yankees fan,
A sucker, I imagined, for my ingenious plan.
With considerable effort, I convinced him to swap,
My **worthless** card for his **priceless** pop.

The bottle's still worth a nickel at the store,
The Mick? I would guess, just a little bit more.
It's displayed on my mantle, like a trophy I earned.
The bitter reminder of a lesson once learned.

The 1952 Rookie Mickey Mantle card has been valued at over $50,000 by some price guides. Wow! I have lots of old baseball cards I collected as a kid, but not this one. How easy it would have been to get a few of them at the time. I wrote this as I watched an old-timer, like a true fisherman, telling a card shop owner about the one that got away.

THE VICTORY

Triumphant at last, I tumbled to the ground.
Slow motion, it seemed as I looked all around.
I lay on my back with my struggles availed.
No need to recount the times I had failed.

I cast out my arms, reached up toward the sky.
With fists clenched tight, I thrust them high.
I screamed out, "Yes!" for victory was mine.
A feeling no words can adequately define.

Tears started flowing, my journey complete.
A magical moment I could never repeat.
Ten thousand times I'd played out this scene.
Never once had I imagined it quite so serene.

They'll say it was luck, as they justify why,
They aren't the ones cheering victory's cry.
The magic reflected in a champion's eyes,
Is the struggle endured to capture their prize.

I'm glad, looking back, for the depth of my pain,
It strengthened my heart and measured my gain.
I've forgotten all those who simply made fun,
Who wonder how I did what "could not be done."

On the journey of success, I was happy to find,
Anyone can do it if they make up their mind.
Whatever envisioned and ventured to achieve,
Is limited only by what you believe.

THE HONOR SYSTEM

It seemed like a logical corner to cut.
I'd fallen into a predictable rut.
When money is a factor, decisions you make
Can mask the importance of what is at stake.

I was treating my Little League baseball team
To an after-game meal, complete with ice cream.
My quick calculation of the ultimate tab,
Provided incentive for an edge I could grab.

I announced to the team, no matter what age,
Kids' meals were listed on the menu's back page.
My goal was to save twenty bucks, maybe more.
An innocent practice I've witnessed before.

When one little boy slowly raised up his hand,
I said to him, "Son, do you not understand?"
"But Coach," he responded, recalling advice,
"Didn't you say, 'Always pay the full price?'

It doesn't seem right to the owner," he said.
"Can I order something that costs less instead?"
I couldn't find words for a moment or two.
It was now crystal clear what I'd asked them to do.

Temptation had clouded my view of the cost.
The money can't measure the honor I lost.
I had to apologize to each of the boys,
And warn them of tricks that evil employs.

TINY AND TANK

Tiny and Tank are inseparable friends.
When one starts to break, the other one bends.
At times they have battled from opposite sides,
When one makes decisions, the other abides.

Tank is a talker, never going unheard.
Tiny, a thinker, barely saying a word.
Tank speaks his mind, no fear and no doubt.
Tiny waits until he has figured things out.

Tank will react without thinking things through.
Tiny contemplates the right thing to do.
Tank is the first to say, "Wow, this is cool."
Tiny must consider if it breaks any rule.

Tank will pursue what he doesn't understand.
Tiny only does what he's carefully planned.
Tank is impatient, easy to distract.
Tiny is persistent, only dealing in fact.

The two are best friends, but you can't always tell;
They don't always work together that well.
Each one is weak where the other is strong.
They have so much to gain if they'd just get along.

Though both seem to come from opposite extremes,
Together they're chasing magnificent dreams.
Tiny and Tank have one common thread,
They both are residing somewhere in my head.

THE RIGHT CHORD

Just taking the stage is a courageous thing,
But I thought to myself, "This lady can't sing."
I was focusing on notes she couldn't quite find,
And timing which dragged just a little behind.
I watched as the audience squirmed all around.
Many were whispering, some even frowned.

I was considering how she had butchered the song,
When it suddenly occurred, I was listening wrong.
So, ignoring the tune, I watched her perform.
Who says all singers should have to conform?
She sang out the words she had hoped we would hear.
Her conviction overshadowed any presence of fear.

She sang with such vigor, excitement, and poise.
I began to appreciate this otherwise noise.
She won't likely sign any record deals soon,
But my heart was touched by her emotional tune.
Her enthusiasm overcame being slightly off-key.
I had learned a great lesson, my mind was set free.

I watched people pass when the service was done,
Unsure what to say, trying not to make fun.
Her smile didn't waiver, as she stood there alone.
Her faith was convicting, her spirit had grown.
When I praised her delivery, I saw her heart melt,
As I thanked her for sharing the passion she felt.

She started shaking my hand and wouldn't let go.
"I'm not the best singer. I really do know."
It was her way of praising the Savior and Lord.
God doesn't care if we find the right chord.

Chapter 5: Creativity (Words)

Creativity: Ingenuity, imagination, ideas, innovation, originality.

"And whatever we ask we receive from Him, because we keep His commandments and do those things that are pleasing in His sight" (1 John 3:22).

What to consider:

- How do you use your creativity to reach others?
- How can the power of words enhance your talent?
- Written or spoken, your words make a difference.

Sheila Stephen Bruce was a high school friend. She has had a remarkable career in music. She is tiny but packs a powerful voice. She was named Miss Indiana in the Miss Indiana Scholarship Pageant. She and her band, The Rodeo Monkeys, perform shows throughout Indiana. She was also the pride of Indiana as she appeared as the mop lady at Hoosier basketball events (if you're from Indiana you know what this means). She uses her voice to inspire others through her radio show, her writing, and her music. She cowrote one of Reba McEntire's number-one hit country singles. She is the proud mother of two boys, and her walk with Christ is evident in her words.

You can visit Sheila on her Facebook artist page: www.facebook.com/sheila.stephen.singer

Guest Foreword by Sheila Stephen Bruce

I'm excited to have the opportunity to write a foreword for this chapter of my friend's book. When Kevin asked me to do it, I was a bit stressed about it! I have written songs and social media posts and poems for my sons, but never anything like this. What do I say? What point do I need to make? And then I realized that I just needed to share my passion for the gift that God has blessed me with—writing. I have been told by many people that I have a gift. They say I am a "crafter of words." To me, writing is an adventure, a journey, a spiritual experience, and a soul-cleanser. Whether I'm writing about a funny moment I've had with my boys and posting it on social media or penning a number-one hit song, it's the same. Writing is comforting and exhilarating at the same time.

Words—they are amazing, aren't they? They can paint a picture. Make you laugh or cry. They are beautiful and healing. They can also be a sharp knife, cutting through your very soul, when used as a weapon. I thank God every day for words. Without them, not only would we not be able to communicate, we would not be able to express, honor, share, praise, or comfort. I'm grateful to have a creative spirit and the gift of writing. I ask God for guidance in everything I write and that He will give me the words He wants me to share with others. In all things, His will be done. I also ask Him to bless this book and its writer. Kevin is a prolific writer who has been blessed with the ability to take words, braid them together with God's Word, and create beautiful poems that impact readers in a very profound way. And finally, I pray that *you* will be blessed by this book—that it will strengthen your relationship with God and others in your life. I hope you find something here that leads you home.

—

POWERFUL WORDS

God gave us the power to have what we say.
Yet we simply speak what we have anyway.
If we trust in His Word and speak what we need,
Satan is forced to comply and concede.

God gave us the power through words that we speak,
To walk in His strength and never be weak.
The words that we say are seeds that we sow.
Whatever we plant is the crop that will grow.

If we talk about things that keep going wrong,
We'll continue to sing the same old sad song.
If we speak of how everything's working out well,
Situations around us will then start to gel.

If we speak of the journey, not ruts in the road,
We'll find strength to handle the heaviest load.
We must speak of our goals as if they were done,
Talk about victory before we have won.

Tell ourselves things we must stretch to achieve.
If we hear it enough, we'll start to believe.
Our brain takes it in, like any other news;
Fate is determined by words that we choose.

God gave us His Word. He promised it's so.
If we follow His guidance, He will not say no.
The secret of life: we create what we say.
It's biblical law. God made us that way.

WORDS DO MATTER

Allegiance, Loyalty, Passion, and Pride:
Words that stir up emotions inside.
Faith, Conviction, Commitment, and Hope:
Words that can help you be able to cope.

Character, Compassion, Heart, and Soul:
Words that assist you in reaching your goal.
Determination, Perseverance, Trust, and Vision:
Words that will lead you to make a decision.

Ambition, Courage, Effort, and Prayer:
Words that can help you arrive anywhere.
Honor, Patriotism, Peace, and Love:
Words that assist you in rising above.

Joy, Laughter, Happiness, and Fun:
Words that will give you the energy to run.
Words do matter. What things do you say?
Your words can change the world every day.

Words will breathe life into all that you do.
They keep you inspired with a positive view.
God gave us the power with words to create,
A way to determine our very own fate.

The best words you'll ever be able to hear:
Words of the Father you'll always hold dear.
"You've followed My Word, accepted My Son.
My good faithful servant, I tell you, well done!"

THE POETIC GRIN

It's turned to a game called "the Poetic Grin."
Mischievous? Maybe, but not quite a sin.
The goal is to catch someone slightly off guard.
If you remain in control, it's not very hard.

There are no certain rules, no victory to take.
Embarrassing your friend is the outcome at stake.
It's best with those you've not seen in a while.
It starts when you flash them a masquerade smile.

As small talk begins, you're setting the bait.
The best strategy is to patiently wait.
"Whatcha been up to?" they'll usually ask.
That's when you put on the "innocent" mask.

"Oh, not much, well…there is one thing.
I've been writing poetry since early last spring.
I think it's my ticket to fortune and fame!"
The next one to speak then loses the game.

You've painted them in with nowhere to go.
You had to be joking, but they don't really know.
From puzzled responses to priceless retorts.
Most can't hold back as laughter resorts.

"Get out!" they'll say. "You're pullin' my sleeve."
Respond with, "Is it really that hard to believe?"
Give them that face like your feelings are hurt.
"You don't like poetry?" softly assert.

Then watch them retreat, not knowing what's true.
Making fun is not something they wanted to do.
They'll likely say something like, "Poetry's nice.
I've read a few poems, maybe once, maybe twice."

The look that they give you can be so much fun.
Confusion will tell you, the game has been won.
It's then you will flash them "the Poetic Grin."
They'll never know whether to believe you again.

WHAT SAY THE WORD?

"Then God said, "Let there be light";
And there was light" (Genesis 1:3).
"Then God said, "Let us make man in Our image, According to Our
likeness"" (Genesis 1:26).
If God created the world with words that He spoke,
And the Bible says we were created in His image,
What are we creating with the words we speak?

If you take anything from this book, this is the message God wants you to hear. There is a creative force in the power of the tongue. You need something to change? Change the way you speak about it. He tells us, if you *believe*, the mountain before you will move, but first you must *tell* it to move.

The difference in failing or finding success
Is found in the words you choose to confess.

PURSUIT OF A POETRY PRIZE

If your ultimate goal is a poetry prize,
There are things you must do without compromise.
I had entered some work at considerable cost,
With no clue at all as to why I had lost.

So I read all the ones recognized in the past,
Seeking form and design for words I could cast.
That's when I discovered a key to their prose:
Illogical thoughts in unorganized rows.

You begin with an outlandish, irrelevant line,
Then something arbitrary to confuse the design.
Like, "In the beginning the ending was near"
Or "We basked in an ardent recollection of fear."

Conclude with some incomprehensible phrase,
Like, "The prolific embrace of our foregone days."
Don't finish ideas in these literary events,
And avoid any phrases that somehow make sense.

What they don't understand, becomes a deep thought.
In depth they will ponder the meaning you sought.
They'll scoff if you've written a limerick or rhyme,
Then cast it aside as a waste of their time.

I'll likely be banned, or be forced to concede,
But I'm sharing the secret it takes to succeed.
Don't stress about structure, don't fret over flow,
Use thoughts you don't have, and words you don't know.

I once had a publisher, who after reading a few of my stories, told me I was too "Dr. Seuss-y." I replied, "Seriously?" I thought, *You mean, **the** Dr. Seuss, seller of like a billion dollars in rhyming poetry?* All I could think to respond was, "Thank you, thank you very much!"

IN BETWEEN THE LINES

The words that I write, the stories I tell,
Sometimes to provoke, sometimes to compel,
Are filled with ideas and unmarked signs,
Lessons in life, folded in between lines.

It's not that I have all the answers, you see,
I'm crafting the soul that resides within me.
More often than not, the moral or theme,
Is not as straightforward as first it may seem.

Sometimes, I simply describe what I saw,
Conclusions I leave for the reader to draw.
Some may be subtle, some may be bold,
Some are just words that need to be told.

Unconventional thoughts in unusual ways;
Simple ideas in a memorable phrase:
Something profound, or a theory proposed,
Or maybe a solution documented in prose.

No matter the reason or purpose within,
No matter the motive for words that I pen,
I pray in between the lines that you read,
You discover whatever you possibly need.

IF I COULD...

If I could write something the whole world might read,
I'd hope to write something that most people need.
It might be some thoughts on the steps of success,
Or maybe a way we can deal with our stress.

Maybe some thoughts about husbands and wives,
Something significant that changes their lives.
It could be some clever, adorable phrase:
Something so witty they'll remember for days.

A screenplay or novel with suspense and romance,
Or what we should do when we're given a chance.
Something that captures their hearts in a way,
To move them to tell someone they know today.

The secrets of life, profoundly revealed,
Or answers to questions discreetly concealed.
It could be a story of strong versus weak,
Or make them aware of the words that they speak.

Something to deal with the thing they most fear:
The fact that for all of us, death with appear.
I thought long and hard about what I should write,
Then realized the answer was right it my sight.

For all that will be or has ever occurred
Has already been written in God's Holy Word.
So if I'd write something the whole world would read,
I'd write down: *The Bible* is all that you need.

My daughter's fourth grade teacher inspired "A Timely Connection." I expect it to happen someday.

A TIMELY CONNECTION

A letter arrived in my mailbox today.
The edges were tattered and starting to fray.
The handwriting that of a child, I would guess.
Curiosity consumed me, I had to confess.

The envelope, colored in purple and black,
A smiley-face sticker was sealing the back.
It was vaguely familiar, like something I knew.
The return name was vacant, providing no clue.

Inside were three pages, each of them filled;
The paper had yellowed like coffee had spilled.
"Who could have written this?" I thought as I read,
The first line exclaiming, "I'm glad you're not dead."

Explaining the task his teacher had made,
A fifth-grader was seeking a prominent grade.
The assignment was to write his hopes and dreams,
To hold nothing back and to think in extremes.

My mind was intrigued as I read through the text.
What would this imaginative kid think of next?
Naïvely optimistic, no thought of constraint,
No excuses were made, no whines, or complaints.

Eager and confident with a soft charming style,
Such words of belief, I've not heard in a while.
I too, was a dreamer with great things in mind,
But the world has distractions, as I'd come to find.

I found myself jealous of this ten-year-old child,
So full of potential with hopes undefiled.
My thought was, I wonder what this kid will do?
How hard will he fight for his dreams to come true?

There was something about him I seemed to relate.
This new-found connection seemed driven by fate.
Somehow he had touched me, I wasn't sure why.
I prayed I could help and committed to try.

He had triggered a passion, ignited a flame,
So I turned the back page to discover his name.
I found there a note that his teacher had signed,
"I send you the dreams that *you* once designed."

That's when it hit me, some thirty years past,
Why I remembered these words that were cast.
She provided the chance to look back and see,
The desires of my heart in a letter from me.

ANGELIC VOICES

One year for Christmas, my mom gave our granddaughter a recordable *'Twas the Night Before Christmas* book. Mom and Dad recorded their voice on every other page. A few years later, after Mom had passed, Haley (then six) was listening to the book. She recognized Great-grandpa's voice but asked who the other voice was. When we told her it was "Nanny Pace," her big brown eyes sparkled with the magic of childlike faith as she innocently asked, "All the way from heaven?"

MERE WORDS

Mere words was the phrase cascading my mind,
As I patiently waited for a break I could find.
He hadn't said anything I did not expect.
I might have agreed had he earned my respect.
But, since he was always so full of advice,
I rarely would ever, if even, think twice.

But this time I stopped to consider the way,
That others respond to what I have to say.
Do I speak in a way that will cause them to feel
That I truly do care, that my feelings are real?
Do I choose my words so as not to condemn
In a way that encourages and edifies them?

Do I temper my words before they come out?
Am I certain of that which I'm talking about?
Do I make them defensive, agendas aside,
Question their character or threaten their pride?
Is the message I offer straightforward and clear,
Or simply *mere words* they will choose not to hear?

The power we don't always know we possess
Is the power that comes from words we confess.

There are those who know things I still need to learn.
There are those who know things not my concern.
What I've learned in my quest for the knowledge I seek,
Is I don't learn a thing by hearing me speak.

Chapter 6: Inspiration

Inspiration: Stimulated, happiness, feeling, generosity, encourage, influence, stir.

"All scripture is given by inspiration of God, and is profitable for doctrine, for reproof, for correction, for instruction in righteousness" (2 Timothy 3:16).

What to look for in this chapter:

- It's great to be inspired; it's another thing to be an inspiration.
- What things or people inspire you the most?
- Does being inspirational have to do with your attitude?
- Are you building others up or tearing them down with your words?

Nikki Lewallen is one of the most positive inspirational people you will ever meet. You cannot have a conversation with her and not come away feeling better about yourself. She is the ultimate encourager. Nikki is a Christian, a wife, a friend to many, and an entrepreneur. She is committed to inspiring people to find their true potential through doing what they love. She is particularly energized to help more people love Mondays. Nikki has spent the past ten years building a membership community called Rainmakers, an organization that supports aspiring and seasoned entrepreneurs to build key relationships and gain the education they need to be successful. For more information, see www.gorainmakers.com.

Guest Foreword by Nikki Lewallen

Rainmakers is a platform that allows me to meet passionate and loving human beings like Kevin and Marla Pace. A very fond memory of mine was when Kevin and Marla received an award in our community for their unique ability to make everyone around them feel special through the work they do and the way they live their lives. They inspire me to be a better Christian, and I cherish the time that I get to spend with them, learning and growing. I am thankful to have many encouraging *Words Do Matter* sayings around my home and office, and I am happy to be a supporter of their success.

I am truly convicted to inspire people to their true potential. Each and every one of us is a miracle from God. Think about it—God knew us from the moment we were conceived. He knew every hair on our head. Science makes us out to be insignificant, like grains of sand on a massive beach. God, however, sees each of us as a marvelously unique human being. Each and every one of us was made to make an impact here on earth. We all have gifts that are meant to be given to others, and those talents energize us to be better individuals. Some people find their unique talents early in life and some not until much later, but it is never too late. You were meant for greatness. You were meant to live a full life of joy and abundance. Find the most inspiring person in your network and reach out for some encouragement or be that person for others. We all have the capacity to do great inspirational things, despite any perceived limitations. We all have a story to tell. How can you be an inspiration to others today?

—Nikki Lewallen

Chapter 6: Inspiration

Early on I learned the value of working hard. My dad was a professor at Indiana University. My mom was a stay-at-home mom. I was the oldest of four kids. Eventually my parents made money, but it wasn't prevalent when I was growing up. I really didn't even notice. I started a paper route at age twelve. It was my first real venture into entrepreneurship. It was a seven-day-a-week commitment. When the bundle of papers came, I either started walking with my pouch, folding and banding papers on the way, or I'd take off on my bike. I had to knock on doors once a week and collect the money. The newspaper company billed me regardless of what I collected. I got to know my customers very well.

> If you know in your heart your dream will prevail,
> You won't even consider the chance you may fail.
> Then falling behind won't make you concede,
> For the heart of a champion is made to succeed.

My customers, for the most part, were all very pleasant and supportive. They even helped me win a local grocery store promotion that sent me to Disneyland in California. I had a pretty good-sized route, and with all of their receipts I ended up coming in second. The trip was an awesome experience.

There were quite a few characters on my route. Sam was one who made an impact. He always greeted me at the door in his wheelchair. There were times I would dread it, because I wanted to get back to a ballgame, but for the most part I politely listened. At the time, his words did not really sink in. Later on, his words would resonate in many things that I did. This is Sam's story:

A MATTER OF INCHES

A proud Army veteran, whose injury claimed,
The use of his legs, yet his heart still remained.
Sam was the last on my newspaper route.
He always was explaining, "What life's all about."

I was barely fourteen and a little naïve.
Things he would tell me were hard to conceive.
I would see him there waiting, hoping to talk.
At times I saw tears as he wished he could walk.

He'd tell me, "Life offers you no guarantees."
He was always polite: thank you and please.
He loved to tell stories, with always, "One more."
He'd patiently wait just inside of his door.

"Life is a matter of inches," he'd say.
"An inch to the left, I'd be standing today.
On the other hand, son, an inch to the right,
And I would have met the Creator that night."

A hundred times over, he asked me it seems,
If I could explain and envision my dreams.
"Things can change quickly, you must understand.
Life doesn't always turn out as you planned."

Then came the day, the sirens would blare.
I ran to the door, but Sam wasn't there.
"He'd fallen," I heard one paramedic say,
"His phone just a matter of inches away."

A week passed by, a note from his wife,
Thanked me for bringing such joy to his life.
"He cherished each day, the time that you took.
He wrote you a message inside of this book."

The old tattered Bible Sam kept in his chair,
"Rejoice, my young friend. I am walking on air!
I leave you this treasure, I expect you to read.
An inch of God's Word is all you will need."

TRUTH ABOUT THE TRUTH

"The *truth* sets us free," or so we've all heard.
Many will quote it from God's Holy Word.
But, fact is, that's not how the Bible verse reads.
The truth by itself doesn't fill any needs.

If you go to the source, John eight: thirty-two,
Then read for yourself what God says is true,
Before any freedoms the truth might achieve,
You must *know* the truth, then choose to believe.

OLD GLORY

Her edges are frayed from battles hard fought.
Her colors are faded from freedoms hard sought.
The lines on her face have been weathered and worn.
The fabric that holds her is tattered and torn.
But she will not harbor or mask alibis;
By God's precious grace, Old Glory still flies.

You must weigh the fear of being denied
Against fear it will work, yet you never tried.

GO CHANGE IT

If we go and ask God to try and explain,
The reason for suffering, heartache, and pain;
His answer won't be an answer at all,
But a challenge, a purpose, a duty, a call.

When evil descends with intent to devour,
God says, "Go change it," that we have the power.
He set the example; He showed us the way.
He gave us authority through words that we say.

Our courage grows stronger from trials we face.
Our spirit is strengthened by running the race.
So rather than give us the things we desire,
He gives us the tools that we will require.

Faith can transform those questioning, "Why?"
Into spiritual warriors who are willing to try,
Into armored believers unwilling to hear
The voices of demons delivering fear.

We can bask in our troubles, bathe in our woes,
Or praise God for challenges, struggles, and blows.
We can whine and complain of how life is unfair,
Or go change the world with the words we declare.

The best way for you to *go change* your circumstances is to give your life to Jesus Christ. His grace can change whatever trials you are facing.

DO YOU HAVE A DREAM?

It was some kind of personal mission he had,
To make sure that no one around him was sad.
He carried a gift, the ability to relate.
A brotherly bond he could instantly create.

He could magically change his personality style,
Greeting each person with a genuine smile.
He loved to say, "Hey, do you have a dream?"
As if from the top of his head it would seem.

He'd shout, "Why on earth not?" at first hesitation.
"You're God's precious child, with a pure destination."
He would never let any opportunity go by.
I asked him about it, he explained to me why.

He told me, "I pray for our Father to place
Those who need hope somewhere in my space.
I made Him a promise by putting them there,
I'd stick out my hand and show them I care.

I pray I'm a blessing to someone today.
When I am, it comes back in a wonderful way."
I spent a day with him, observed what he did;
With childlike faith, he would act like a kid.

Amazing how few could tell him their dream.
"An epidemic," he called it, "of low self-esteem."
But, somehow he'd manage to get them to think,
"Hold on to your dream! Do not let it sink!"

He never met a stranger, and remembered each name.
He's home now in heaven, surely doing the same.
Angels should be ready with answers I suppose,
They won't be exempt from the question he'll pose.

They'd best answer quickly or likely get caught,
"Do you have a dream? Why in heaven not?"
With an angelic smile, he'll shout from his star,
"You need a big dream, wherever you are!"

I worked at a grocery store though high school and college. During those grocery store days, I began coming out of my shell and gaining confidence. I quickly adapted to the work environment as a sophomore in high school. I got the job when I was getting milk for my mom. I ran across the store manager who recognized me from Little League baseball. It was a busy day when he asked me if I wanted a job. I wasn't even done shrugging my shoulders when he handed me an apron and marched me up front to bag groceries. A two-minute training drill, a call to Mom to say, "Guess what?" and suddenly I was part of the working class. It turned out to be a very good job. I moved from bagger to stocker to assistant manager on certain shifts. That job paid my entire way through college without any loans or financial aid.

I met Dan one day at the grocery store. Dan owned a floor cleaning business. Dan walked in and asked me where he could find the manager. "Good luck!" I told him, knowing the manager did not always treat salesman with a joyous heart. That's when he told me, "Luck's not involved when you know how to pray." I had never met anyone so bold in their faith. I knew he was right, having given my life to Jesus at age twelve, but I had never really talked about it much. I worked the night shift that evening and without thinking relayed the story to the crew. Now the night shift crew could be, putting it nicely, kind of rough. They nicknamed Dan "Church-boy" in an unflattering way. I felt bad because I respected the way he shared his faith. I apologized to him for what I had done, but it didn't bother him in the least. In fact, none of the badgering bothered him. He just put on that big smile and said, "God still loves you." I always looked forward to working when Dan was there. He helped me through more things than he will ever know.

CHURCH-BOY

I held back a chuckle when he strolled in the store,
Explaining God sent him to clean up our floor.
There was something about him, a confident air,
A magical grin, and an eye-to-eye stare.

I was eighteen years old and working my way
Through college stocking shelves at the local I.G.A.
I wished him good luck at the manager's door,
Where I'd seen many salesmen get tossed out before.

He said, "Luck's not involved if you know how to pray."
I knew he was right, but had started to stray.
I was working the graveyard shift later that week,
It wasn't the place for the mild or the meek.

Some crusty old timers worked that time of night.
Like a school of piranha, just waiting to bite.
On his very first night, the word quickly spread,
They nicknamed him Church-Boy from what I had said.

I prayed he was ready for the wolves to attack.
I watched his reactions; he didn't step back.
He boldly responded, "Do you know the Lord?"
Deflecting each comment like wielding a sword.

I admired his courage and passionate desire.
I admired his conviction, his faith, and his fire.
Halfway through the shift, he entered my aisle.
He brought me some coffee and talked for a while.

"I noticed you didn't join in with the rest.
The bashing of Church-Boy the biblical pest."
"I'm sorry," I said, "I spoke your belief.
I didn't expect them to give you such grief."

He smiled and said, "No, you did the right thing.
You opened the door to the message I bring."

"What message is that?" though I already knew.
He said, "God sent His Son for me and for you!"

A bond was established; a friendship was born.
He helped me stay strong and not to conform.
He kept up his message, stayed true to his walk.
There were so many times that I needed that talk.

Now forty plus years since those grocery store days,
I still can recall one particular phrase.
"You can mock me, hate me, or say I'm uncouth,
But, the fact still remains: I'm telling the truth."

He still spreads the Word on those overnight shifts.
He shares his great faith, that's one of his gifts.
Like a personal angel sent to give me a hand.
Thanks, my friend, Church-Boy, for taking a stand.

DÉJÀ VU

That blasted alarm blared a deafening roar.
I leaped from my bed, down the hole in the floor.
A familiar old memory echoed my mind.
I chased away thoughts I did not want to find.

We screeched to a stop at an old vacant site.
The building engulfed, the flames burning bright.
Our squad was assembled, each person in range.
A system we follow, and don't ever change.

The ground started shaking from a powerful blast.
The heat was intense with the glow that it cast.
As a woman ran out with fire on her clothes,
My instincts took over, my adrenalin rose.

Chapter 6: Inspiration

I tackled and rolled her around in the dirt.
I smothered the flames out before she got hurt.
She was screaming, "My son, my son is inside!"
I turned toward the danger, again we collide.

My prevailing thought now on the son I had lost.
I must save this boy, no matter the cost.
Without giving heed to the system we run,
I burst through the door, my search had begun.

The fury of the flames was laced full of fear.
I yelled my boy's name then listened to hear.
The beams began bending, I felt the floor crack.
The black stench of smoke gave a daunting attack.

I found an old freezer, my hand grabbed the door.
A chill pierced my spine, I had been here before.
As I lifted the lid, he lay perfectly still.
The same way I found my ten-year-old Bill.

I had struggled to forget that horrible sight.
In the heat of the battle I was frozen with fright.
But he opened his eyes as if back from the dead.
"Have you seen my mom?" he then quietly said.

I grabbed up that boy and held on tight.
We ran through the flames, timed it just right.
The ceiling caved in as we dove through the door.
A mom's prayer answered to see him once more.

Stretched out on the ground, my mind wasn't there.
I was off in my world of guilt and despair.
Tears filled my eyes, everything was a blur.
Then softly I heard the kid say, "Thank you, sir."

"Billy said you would come, to not be concerned.
If I hid in that box, I wouldn't get burned."
I still have those moments I question God, "Why?
Why innocent people sometimes have to die?"

The answer eludes me, but through this I've found,
Comfort in knowing his spirit's around.
I'll keep fighting fires, that's just what I do.
That blasted alarm just rang—***déjà vu.***

I wrote "Deja Vu" for my brother-in-law and firefighter, Andy. It started with a line, then the rhyme dictated where it was going. I had no idea where the story would go. It hangs in several firehouses in Indianapolis. God bless our first responders and our soldiers.

A SOLITARY SOLDIER

In the woods by the fort we gathered around.
He mapped out a plan with a stick in the ground.
He spoke about honor, conviction, and pride.
Just like a great coach, he stirred things inside.

"We must stop the enemy from invading our land.
The safety of our nation resides in your hand."
Our illustrious flag I was assigned to patrol,
From a hillside bunker where we'd taken control.

The platoon all dispersed as our mission began.
I took aim with my rifle according to plan.
It was all I could do to not tremble with fear.
What if a sniper snuck up on me here?

I remembered the words the commander had said,
"We'll never give up 'til the last soldier's dead."
The sounds of the battle were beginning to rage,
I gripped tight the trigger, prepared to engage.

A wounded man shouted, "Help, I've been hit."
I tightened my helmet and crouched just a bit.

Chapter 6: Inspiration

Suddenly, I saw them come out from the trees.
I took aim and fired. One fell to his knees.

Another one or two, but soon I could see,
Too many of them against only one me.
With no other choice, I was forced to decide.
So I raced to the flag with gun at my side.

Suddenly the weapon dropped out of my grip.
The thought entered in I won't make it this trip.
I looked at my arm, there was nothing but red.
Then two hit my chest and one grazed my head.

Slow motion it seemed as I fell to the ground.
I wanted to scream but couldn't utter a sound.
Looking up at the stars, the pain was intense.
I was proud of my effort, if that makes any sense.

I knew it was over, I knew we were done.
My countrymen dead, the enemy had won.
As a rebel soldier found my line of sight,
He dangled the flag and danced with delight.

I considered what could be my fate and I sighed,
For the sake of our freedom, how many have died?
He looked down at me and proceeded to say,
"You look pretty bad, you sure you're okay?"

With utter respect for those who go fight,
I looked up and said, "I think I'm all right.
But, that hurt so bad, I thought I would faint!
Good thing these bullets are made out of paint."

No disrespect meant for our fighting soldiers. This is a story that honors
what they go through, with a little twist at the end.

MANSIONS IN HEAVEN

Every day I drive by, gazing up to behold
A breathtaking sight, someone's story untold.
A picturesque setting, a sketch you might see.
A palace surely built for a king to live free.

A majestic log home, a spectacular view,
Overlooking the city, only noticed by few.
The roofline crescendos, a cymbal crashing note.
Windows, like water, seem to shimmy and float.

A signature deck that must stretch all around.
A porch swing calls out for serenity found.
Massive log beams like a heavenly gate,
The glow of the cedar enlightens the estate.

With landscaped perfection, exact and pristine,
No artist could paint a more beautiful scene.
The curve of the wood, like a soft southern quilt,
An awesome design, so masterfully built.

The entry cascades like a gently flowing stream.
This home a fulfillment of somebody's dream.
I too have a dream of constructing such walls.
The doors will be open whenever God calls.

THE MASK

We keep to ourselves, we hide it so well.
These things deep inside, we don't want to tell.
The mask we put on so no one will know,
To hide what we feel, so nothing will show.

They don't recognize this cover we wear,
Concealing the past, so not to compare.
It doesn't come off very much anymore,
From so many times being knocked to the floor.

Lines have been drawn from battles we've lost,
A portrait of pain, a canvas embossed.
It's almost as if it's a part of us now.
A shelter it seems we've accepted somehow.

We've worn it so much that no one can see,
We put on the mask but scream to break free.
Thinking we're strong from all we've been through,
It's simply the mask disguising their view.

Someday we will leave that mask far behind,
Content with ourselves, whatever they find.
It's then we'll discover we've not been alone.
We each have designed a mask of our own.

Chapter 7: Leadership (Success)

Leadership: Encouragement, success, perseverance, prosperity, righteousness, guidance, victory, example.

"For I have given you an example, that you should do as I have done to you" (John 13:15).

What to consider:

- How does leadership affect your success?
- Will you do more for someone else than for yourself?
- Does God want you to succeed?
- How do you help others succeed with your words?

Kenton Yohey has the gift of uplifting people. He has a way of helping people look past their obstacles. He always has a kind word to say. He has created a very successful marketing team. He will be the first to tell you he didn't do it alone. He has surrounded himself with positive, encouraging people. He has become a leader by first being a servant. The true test of leadership is the ability to help create leaders. Kenton and Andre'a have helped raise up many leaders in the community. Today as a couple and parents to their sixteen-year-old son Luke, they continue to build and develop a worldwide marketing business. They also lead the *Christian Phone Book* circulation, which is a thirty-year-old directory of Christian business owners and professionals in central Indiana.

Check out their website www.ChristianPhoneBook.com or the Mobile Christian Phone Book App at http://get.theapp.co/33a9/

Guest Foreword by Kenton Yohey

L eadership is made by example and then influence. Each of us chooses whose example and influence we will follow. The summer before my senior year in college at Indiana University in Bloomington, Indiana, I had an opportunity to meet and work with a group of leaders in business that had a profound impact on my life. With Andre'a, my now wife and partner for thirty-eight years, we started a marketing business with the coaching and mentoring we needed to succeed. As with anything it took work, dedication, and commitment. What we found became more than just a business but also an environment and culture of success, based on principles that changed our lives. Many years ago, we got to know Kevin and Marla on a personal basis and were tremendously inspired by their example and friendship. Their story is one of love and overcoming. Our lives have been touched by their story.

It has been said, "If you're going to walk through a minefield, it's better to follow someone." In life, we must navigate through many treacherous minefields. It is always better to follow someone who has made it through successfully. To be successful in life, we must lead. To lead, we must first follow. Before we follow, we need to make sure of where we want to go and follow others who are going there. I believe God's Word is where all truth, success, and leadership is found. Jesus Christ is the ultimate example to follow. You can be a leader right where you are today. You begin by encouraging those around you. You have a purpose and calling on your life. If you don't know it yet, ask God where and how He wants you to lead. He will answer. Remember, your *words do matter,* so choose them carefully.

—Kenton Yohey

THE "DON'T DO IT!" CAFÉ

So many ideas swim around in your head,
Then someone else takes them to market instead.
Some good and some bad, some hot and some cold,
Some with potential to really take hold.

Unfortunately most don't make it too far,
Lost while they search for the next shooting star.
That great inspiration, now fleeting away,
From a visit to the famous "Don't do it!" café.

Advice is free-flowing, but the prices are high,
As stalwart old patrons explain to you why.
Adverse to the changes they've seen over time,
They'll try to convince you that poems don't rhyme.

But, they have been wrong many times in the past.
Remember them, saying, "Computers won't last?"
In fact, thinking back, there rarely has been
An idea considered they concluded could win.

They'll still be your friends, but consider the source.
Should they be the ones to determine your course?
Trust in your instincts and stay far away,
From the specials at the famous "Don't do it!" café.

THAT WHICH WON'T MOVE

What in the world was I trying to prove,
Pushing the thing that won't possibly move?
"It's crazy," they said. I've heard that before.
Their negative thoughts kept me pushing for more.

107

As I pushed over time, and they plainly could see
The thing that they said, "Could not possibly be,"
Was moving despite all the wisdom advised,
"It had to be luck," was the answer devised.

Seems that which I moved wasn't nearly as strong
As for them to admit they were possibly wrong.
It's possible though, the thing that I proved,
Is for them, they were right, it cannot be moved.

A STARK REVELATION

From stage I had witnessed him speak on success.
He had written a book on the words we confess.
I remembered having bought it, a couple years back.
It sits on my books-I-should-read-someday stack.

Then one day I met him in the aisle of a store.
We seemed to establish an instant rapport.
He listened intently as I rambled about—
My thoughts not defined, my words full of doubt.

I exclaimed, "I'm a writer of poetry and prose.
I'm just getting started. We'll see how it goes."
The typical response I had gotten used to
Was a no-explanation cynical view.

But this gentleman looked me square in the eye.
"You'll never succeed at something you try."
The puzzled expression I must have conveyed,
Was like bluffing when all my cards had been played.

He explained that, "Success is not stumbled upon.
Without a commitment, it soon would be gone.

If you wrote a book with the words you just spoke,
You could call it a lesson on how to be broke."

He then shook my hand and gave me a wink.
"Words that you say form thoughts that you think."
I stood there, dumbfounded for a moment or two,
Amazed at what he had been able to do.

With a few choice words, precisely delivered,
He showed a perspective I had never considered.
The challenges I blamed for making me stressed,
Were placed there by me through words I confessed.

Sometimes it's not the words that you say
But the way that you say them that gets in the way.

There are moments like these that separate those
Who no one remembers or everyone knows.

Something inside you will seek to disprove
The notion that anything, "Simply won't move."

If you're constantly looking for corners to cut,
And your *why* explanations include the word *but*.
The harvest you hoped from seeds you had sown,
May not be all that could have been grown.

A VIEW FROM THE VALLEY

In anguish one day I asked God to defend
His reason for not letting all of this end.
Each challenge I faced would merely bring more;
This battle-scarred warrior was losing the war.

I'd look all around, everywhere I could see
Were those who were prospering much more than me.
Through trials and struggles, heartache and pain,
It seemed like my efforts had all been in vain.

With little hope left, I was weary and tired.
I screamed out, "Dear God, what more is required?"
So I asked a good friend who had been through a lot,
"How did you make it through battles you fought?"

She explained that with every setback she faced,
She kept praising God and her fear was erased.
"If you don't even praise Him through serious blows,
Then who will you praise when success overflows?"

Perseverance breeds character, integrity, and trust.
Passion is strengthened when you do what you must.
God gave you a gift, a dream, and a goal,
But, just like a diamond, it's wrapped up in coal.

When you glorify God through trials you face,
Your faith will empower the gift of His grace.
Then when the world stands up to applaud,
You'll understand why, and give it to God.

110

THE NEED TO SUCCEED

I'd watched him succeed at whatever he tried,
While all of my chances eventually died.
He liked to goof off; he liked to have fun.
I focused my time on getting things done.

In quiet desperation, my patience grew thin.
At the height of frustration, I finally gave in.
I threw up my arms, tossed ego aside.
I lowered my walls and swallowed my pride.

I asked him to help me to understand how.
I'd embrace any wisdom he'd care to endow.
I've searched for so long to find what it takes,
But I seem to keep making consistent mistakes.

My thought was: I just want to prove that I can.
If he taught me the steps, I'd follow the plan.
Looking straight in my eyes, he squinted to see,
As if he were searching for something in me.

He thought for a moment, then chuckled and said,
"Look with your heart and not with your head."
I must have looked puzzled, or dazed and confused.
So he told me the secret that he'd always used.

"When that which you want is that which you need,
You'll discover how easy it is to succeed.
You won't find the answer in how hard you try,
You'll figure out *how*, when you understand *why*."

HYPNOTIC SUGGESTION

WARNING: The following story could render you powerless to excuses. This type of hypnosis should only be performed by registered poets. Proceed with caution!

A swinging gold watch on a path you can trace,
A monotonous, compelling, and repetitive pace,
The journey begins to the depths of your mind,
The shackles that hold you begin to unwind.

Peace wraps around you as thoughts start to flee;
A solitude imagined as your body breaks free.
Now totally relaxed, your eyelids like stone,
Your sole concentration on words being sown.

You're feeling receptive to what is confessed,
Your directive is, "Follow what I now suggest."
Whenever you happen to hear the word *can't*,
Your look will be puzzled. Your head will slant.

In searching your mind the word won't be found.
You'll barely be able to process the sound.
You'll reply with, "I'm sorry, I must not have heard.
Did you say *can't*? That's not a real word."

You'll chase after dreams without holding back;
That miserable phrase won't throw you off track.
At the snap of my fingers, you'll wake up to find
Can't won't be something that enters your mind.

SNAP!

112

SIMPLY DECIDE

The typical comment was, "That teacher's weird."
I was assigned to her class just as I feared.
She wasn't afraid to get right in your face.
She never called me Kevin, always, "Mr. Pace."

She would not let you slack, would not let you slide.
She spoke about character, honor, and pride.
They said she was hard, radical, and mean.
Love her or hate her, there were few in between.

Our convictions were tested on the very first day.
She opened our thoughts to think in a way
That others don't consider or might never try,
To challenge what we see, always questioning why.

She wrote on the board to "Simply decide."
Her words began stirring up thoughts deep inside.
What was she saying? We did not understand.
"Decide what?" someone asked, raising their hand.

Pausing for a moment, while stroking her chin,
"That's all up to you, but it's time you begin."
Most blew her off as elusive and strange,
But I chose to listen, expecting to change.

I wrote down some things that motivated me,
Sketched out some dreams that I wanted to see.
My thought was, Pursue and not simply react.
I kept my mind focused and wholly intact.

I mapped out a plan with specific details;
I readied my ship and hoisted my sails.
It served as my senior project that year.
She said, "Mr. Pace, what do we have here?

It appears you've decided just as I had asked.
Very few understood that remedial task.
I challenge you now, like never before,
To look deep inside and begin to explore.

For whatever road you may choose to take,
Success is a choice, a decision you make."
I returned a few times to see her at school.
She still called me mister, her unbroken rule.

I spoke at her funeral, a celebration event.
She knew exactly what price had been spent.
For carved on her stone, just as on her board,
"I simply decided to follow the Lord."

I wrote this about a remarkable fifth grade teacher I had. Though the story is fiction, her impact was not.

The first ones to quit are the first ones to say,
"They never will quit," then they just fade away.

DESPERATION'S DOOR

When things don't work out the way that you thought,
And you feel disheartened from battles you've fought,
When victory seems to be so far away,
And hope overshadowed from thoughts of dismay,
That's when it shines like never before,
Opportunity knocks on desperation's door.

114

COURAGE OR FEAR?

He said, "It takes courage to do what you do."
I said, "It's not courage from my point of view."
"Fear," I told him, "has a greater effect
On things that I do, or things I neglect."

For anyone watching, it's perfectly clear,
I tend to avoid doing things that I fear.
It doesn't take courage for an eagle to soar,
For a champion to play, or a lion to roar.

It's not even courage that makes someone brave,
Fear may be driving the way they behave.
They'll watch as you rise like a champion would,
Then call you courageous; they've misunderstood.

AN EAGLE WILL FLY

There are times, as a friend, you tie someone's shoes.
There are times, as a leader, when you have to refuse.
There are those you can teach, those willing to learn.
There are others who will not embrace that concern.

There are those who will say that they want to succeed,
Who will talk a good game but then simply concede.
There are few who will listen and heed your advice,
Who don't start to question each tool or device.

They'll likely not be the ones you had thought
Would always stick by you, successful or not.
It's the ones who are able to see past your flaws,
The ones who with passion believe in the cause.

For the lack of a dream makes it easy to quit.
Casting excuses, whatever might fit;
Just remember, no matter how often you try
To toss up a chicken—it never will fly.

SMILING INSIDE

They'll brazenly scoff, "It cannot be done."
Inside you will smile. Why spoil their fun?
Once you step forward, despite their advice,
Comments will cease. That's them thinking twice.

They've seen other people succeeding before.
You've made them uneasy by striving for more.
It's not that they don't believe that it's true.
It's been done before, just never by you.

Once progress is shown toward meeting your plan,
They'll say, "It won't last. It's a flash in the pan."
When they ask, "How's it going?" It's just a façade.
If you grimace, they'll give you that head-bobbing nod.

When ultimate success becomes painfully clear.
"It was luck"—the conclusion you'll generally hear.
In time they'll concede, "It was simply a joke,"
Attempting to change the words that they spoke.

"We knew you could do it. We've always believed.
We proudly support the things you've achieved."
They'll jump on the wagon as if they had scored.
Inside you will smile, and say, "Welcome aboard."

One of the best motivators is being told you cannot do something. Your victory wouldn't be a story if you did not have to struggle through it. Your struggle won't become a victory if you listen to the naysayers and allow them to steal your dream.

THE *DO THEY* SIGN

How far will you go in the quest for your dream?
Do they call you a radical, say you're extreme?
Have they started complaining you're totally obsessed?
Do they claim to be worried you don't seem to rest?

Do they give you that look as if they would know
A better way to get to where you want to go?
Do they mention how working so hard is insane?
Why put yourself through such torture and pain?

Do they not comprehend when things seem so clear?
Could it be your success is their genuine fear?
Do they try to convince you of their point of view?
Attempt to place limits on what you can do?

Are you willing to brush all the questions aside?
Is your biggest fear saying, "I wish I had tried"?
If no one has laughed or questioned at all,
It's then you should know—your dream is too small!

Use what they say as motivation to succeed.
Your conviction will cause them to follow your lead.
The first ones to cheer and applaud will be those,
Who thought they knew better! That's just how it goes.

Don't be disillusioned if they don't understand,
Just plan what you do, then do what you planned.

It's a glorious feeling, that look of surprise,
When they watch you succeed in front of their eyes.

WATCH OUT FOR THIEVES

A revealing moment that still hurts to recall.
I discovered my conviction was incredibly small.
I managed to let someone walk on my dream,
Damaging my sometimes too bold self-esteem.

A friend pulled me over and looked in my eyes,
"Do you really believe or just fantasize?"
"What do you mean?" I questioned the thought.
"Look at the battles that we both have fought."

Then came the question to test my desires,
"What if that thief was stealing your tires?"
I thought for a moment, "That can't be the same."
"You're right," the reply, "your car's pretty lame."

"You know you'd protect that broken-down tank.
Which, by the way, is mostly owned by the bank.
You speak of your vision as if you are proud,
Yet 'stealing-your-dream' is somehow allowed?"

My friend was correct, my priorities skewed;
I've now changed the way my treasures are viewed.
I've learned the response that conviction requires.
No one can steal my dream…or my tires.

LEADERSHIP SAYINGS

The twists and turns that tangle our past
Will make up the glory that triumph will cast.

If you rise to the challenge facing your fears,
It's never as bad as it first so appears.

Whether you rise from the heat of the fire
Is dependent upon your depth of desire.

If passion doesn't drive us, then apathy does.
We sacrifice "what is" when we glorify "what was."

It may seem as though we can barely hang on;
One tiny slip and we'll surely be gone.
But remember if ever our hope starts to dim,
the fruit on a tree is out on the limb.

If you think you're too tired, too busy, too stressed,
It could be the words your tongue has confessed.

If you feel overshadowed, lost in the trees,
Embrace the potential that everyone sees.
Fasten your roots and reach for the sky;
Rise with a passion no one can deny.

Do you have a goal, a purpose, a plan,
Or simply responding the best that you can?

Sometimes in order to know what to do,
You have to step back, take a different view.
Sometimes we're too close to the problem to see
What everyone else knows the answer to be.

When things don't work out the way I expected,
It's usually because of a task I neglected.

The illusion of fortune is a camouflaged trap.
It's a one-way ticket on a how-to-fail map.

From rags to riches, the old story goes,
But without the rags, the story just blows.

When so many others can do the same thing,
Why would they listen when you start to sing?
The difference you'll find that will set you apart
Is the passion you carry down deep in your heart.

The test of success is not simply succeed,
It's how many others are you able to lead?

Did you think it was easy, this thing called success?
Everyone would do it if the effort were less.

When you laugh at the storms that bring you such pain,
Fear turns to hope as you dance in the rain.

They say that the view from the top of the hill
Is quiet, serene, peaceful, and still.
If you keep pushing on, enduring the pain,
You'll find that the struggle will measure your gain.

The dream is alive. Get up off the floor.
Spread out your wings like an eagle and soar.

It's not as important where it is you may land,
As it is that you've chosen a place you could stand.

When the storms of life we often must face
Threaten our conviction and hold us in place,
We must learn to stay strong despite any fear;
If we hope to succeed, we must persevere.

I've found that it's not always easy to find
A way to catch up, once you've gotten behind.

I don't want to do something anyone could.
I want to do something that no one else would.

Be careful what corners you cut on the way,
It may lead you somewhere you don't want to stay.

If you want to get better, the best thing to do
Is play against those who are better than you.

The best lessons learned are not when we win,
But when we are willing to stick out our chin.

Sometimes we get stuck in the corner we've found,
When something might change if we'd just turned around.

It's not all about who won or who lost,
Who paid the price, or who counted the cost;
It's more about learning how character defines
The way that a champion's attitude shines.

Momentum depends on what angle you choose,
Are you playing to win or trying not to lose?

It's one of those feelings you never forget,
A last-second shot drawing nothing but net.

The heart of the matter that sets you apart
And defines your success is a matter of heart.

When the height of your logic quickly departs,
Your depth of conviction will stir in their hearts.

The price that you pay is a temporary cost.
The prize that you earn will never be lost.

"Well said," is deserved for those who believe.
"Well done," is reserved for those who achieve.

Though others may run, nowhere to be found,
With strength of conviction, I'm standing my ground.

We fight so that one day our children will see
And then understand what it means to be free.

Be careful the place you decide you will start—
Things garnered easily quickly depart.

Chapter 8: Servanthood (Bible Stories)

Servanthood: Selflessness, empathy, encouragement, faith, humility.

"But many who are first will be last, and the last first."
(Matthew 19:30).

What to consider:

- Jesus taught through the use of parables. How have the stories from the Bible impacted your walk with Him?
- Consider well-known Bible stories from a different point of view. They may bring new meaning.
- What does it mean to truly be a servant?
- Why do we always think we can earn *grace*?

Sarah Scharbrough McLaughlin is a very talented singer/songwriter. She is the daughter of one of my table tennis buddies. Sarah has performed all over the world with her songs of simple faith. She and her husband are busy with five little future musicians. She uses her talents to serve the body of Christ. Her newest album, *Sit with Me,* is awesome! To find more on Sarah's journey with words and music, visit www.sarahtunes.com.

Guest Foreword by Sarah Scharbrough McLaughlin

What an honor to write a foreword to this chapter. As a worship leader, songwriter, and blogger, I am aware of the great power of words. As a wife and mother to five young children, I'm learning that using words to encourage one another may be our greatest service to one another.

I've had the privilege of knowing Kevin and Marla through my parents. My dad and Kevin are friends from playing table tennis together. They've become generous supporters of our art and ministry and encouraging and inspiring friends along the way.

I'll be the first to admit that servanthood does not come naturally for me. It is easy for me to fall into a pattern of thinking I deserve more or that I've earned coming out on top. Perhaps this is a universal struggle to some extent. Choosing to use music and writing to point to the grace of God and choosing to depend on Christ for His love and help as a mother has led me to serve my family, church, and community. Only in this reliance and choice to be generous and hospitable have I seen myself used in the kingdom of God. The line in Kevin's poem "Feed Them" perhaps says it best: "If we'll give just a little, the Lord will provide." Proverbs 11 reminds us that those who refresh others will themselves be refreshed. We have seen time and time again that acting out of service and generosity, the way that Jesus has done, is the best path to peace and love—for both the receiver and giver.

—Sarah McLaughlin

TICKET TO PARADISE

Death's sting now upon me, so clearly in view.
Hope has long vanished. My life is now through.
I always believed I would turn things around.
That doesn't seem likely ten feet off the ground.

This cross holds me captive on public display:
An example for those who choose the wrong way.
Leaving woeful regrets and one fleeting request
That I be forgiven for sins I've confessed.

This man here beside me, the brunt of their rage,
I feel a connection. We share the same stage.
He carried His cross down a cobblestone street.
Soldiers drove nails in His hands and His feet.

I heard the wood splinter from the force of the blow.
What crime was committed? No one seems to know.
A sharp thorny crown is piercing His head.
His battle-scarred face a dark bloodstained red.

His flesh lanced open from a metal-tipped strap,
Lines stripe His back like a fine, detailed map.
They've hung a sign, claiming Him, "King of the Jews."
I have a strange feeling somehow I must choose.

They're shouting, "Break free, if you are the One."
He asked for forgiveness for what they had done.
I've not seen such love and compassion before—
An innocent lamb sacrificed at death's door.

His torn, battered body was abused and defiled,
An unthinkable ending for God's precious Child.
A storm has engaged as lightning bolts dance.
Could this be the end, or simply my chance?

I watched Him, preparing to journey somewhere.
I asked, if He would, to remember me there.
He looked back at me, eyes shining like ice,
"Today you shall join me in sweet paradise."

He said, "It is finished," claimed His last breath—
A Savior who won't be obstructed by death.
A warmth filled my body. My sins were set free.
I watched as He died. It seemed just for me.

To die next to Him, such a strange twist of fate.
The request of this sinner did not come too late.
I made some poor choices, I could not afford,
But my sins were forgiven by Jesus, my Lord!

"Ticket to Paradise" was truly a gift of the Holy Spirit. I woke up one morning, and it all came out in about twenty minutes. I know it was not from me. I felt like all I did was move the pen. I am just glad I had pen and paper on the nightstand. Reflecting on the story, I realized how powerful this interaction with Jesus and the thief really was. So many people and churches get so hung up on procedure—how you do this, or if you did that—often causing great turmoil. To me, this story breaks down all those barriers—the thief expressed his faith in a simple question. Jesus responded, "Today, you will be with me in paradise." It doesn't get any simpler than that. The answer? Faith, simple and childlike faith.

This story came as a challenge from Marla to look at a Bible story from a child's perspective.

"FEED THEM"

It seemed the whole town had shown up that day.
The crowd was enormous, I was fighting my way
To the man they called Jesus, the One I had heard
Could captivate thousands with merely a word.
A basket of food was strapped to my belt,
Not much, but more than most had been dealt.

When I finally reached Him, I sat on the ground.
Some men were there talking, all gathered around.
I'd heard of the rumors: He could be God's Son.
Their concern was about how to feed everyone.
So I raised up my hand, standing up to declare,
"I have some food, you're all welcome to share."

Jesus then turned His focus on me.
"Your generous heart has just set you free."
He lifted my basket of food toward the sky.
"Feed them!" He said to those standing by.
They didn't understand His commandment at all.
"Feed this large crowd with a basket so small?"

But they served up the food to everyone there,
Amazed to find out there was plenty to spare.
Then Jesus knelt, placed His hand on my heart.
"Thank you, young man, for doing your part."
The lesson He taught me, I use as my guide,
If we'll give just a little, the Lord will provide.

BLUEBERRY SURPRISE

One of our favorite stories happened at the Blueberry Festival in Plymouth, Indiana. It is not a "look at what we did" story, it is a "look at what God did" story. It was our first time doing this show, and we ended up in a tent without much traffic. This particular show was extremely difficult to set up and take down because the vendors seemed to bottleneck at a certain point. We became friends with some neighboring vendors who made candles. Their candles were high quality, but there was an abundance of candle makers at the show. Our friends were realizing the difficulties competition brings.

The wife came to our booth over and over again, connecting on an emotional level. She was intrigued by a large framed print we call "The Gift." The print itself is a close up of Jesus' hand on the cross with the reflection of the crucifixion on the spike. It is a very powerful piece that often doesn't present itself at first. Many people are unsure what they are seeing at first. We sometimes have to help them see it. The look of astonishment on their faces when the picture *pops* out at them is priceless. She brought countless people to show them the picture. She had shared with us a little about having money issues and her promise to her husband to not buy anything at this show.

As the end of the show drew near my meds were wearing off, and we knew how difficult tear-down would be. It was a few hours before closing when the candle lady graciously gave us a few candles to show her appreciation. That situation is always somewhat awkward. Do you reciprocate or honor their gracious intentions? After she left, we discussed it. Marla's giving heart quickly came up with the idea of giving her the big picture that she so adored. My accountant brain quickly took over. It was an expensive picture, priced at $250 ($60 cost). I reasoned, "We haven't done that well at this show." As my words were coming out, I knew she was right. We agreed if it didn't sell, we would give it to her. After we made the decision, we were strangely excited about *not* selling it.

When the time came, Marla walked the picture to their booth. There was another couple sitting with them, so she hesitated, then motioned to the wife. She immediately knew Marla's intentions and started shaking her head, tears filling her eyes. It was an emotional exchange as Marla, in her special way, convinced them to accept the gift. We included a story card about how they could impact the world with their faith.

When Marla returned, it was time to start packing up for the long journey ahead. About that time, a college-age kid came into our booth and was very interested in our work. We rarely sell anything to college kids; they don't have the space. So, I have to admit, given the time constraint I was reluctant to get into a deep conversation. Finally, as I suspected, he wandered off. Then the candle lady came back in tears, obviously shaken. "What's wrong?" Marla asked. She explained that the couple with them were her in-laws, and her father-in-law was a non-believer. She said when he read the card he was moved to tears. It soon became one huge cry-fest.

With the show now over, the college kid showed up again with two of his buddies. *Great,* I thought, *another distraction.* Well, it didn't take long, and those three young kids bought over $600 in pictures—ten times what we had in the one we gave away. I've seen God work in our lives many times, but rarely so quickly and with such a recognizable response. Then, the three offered to help us tear down and haul stuff out to our truck (which was almost a mile away). God is so good!

THE ARMOR OF GOD

We live in a world where evil is free,
Free to confuse the things that we see.
In the valley of death where demons will trod,
Put on the armor, the armor of God.

Put on the helmet. Pick up the sword.
Join in the battle and follow the Lord.
Don't be deceived by Satan's façade!
Put on the armor, the armor of God.

The shield will hold your enemies at bay.
The spirits must honor the words that you say.
Go forth in praise, in worship, and laud:
Put on the armor, the armor of God.

This plate will defend your chest from a blow.
No weapon formed against you will grow.
No longer fooled by deception or fraud,
Put on the armor, the armor of God.

The armor of God is the faith that we wear.
Adorned by the words we've chosen to snare.
The suit is complete with staff and rod;
Put on the armor, the armor of God.

Providing protection from heavenly loss,
Secured by a Savior, sacrificed on a cross,
Triumphantly angels will stand to applaud
when you put on the armor, the armor of God.

David was one of God's unlikely messengers. I can imagine people laughing at the brash, overconfident kid, willing to do what none of them was willing to do. When he shed his armor, they must have mocked him even more. I would have loved to have seen the looks on their faces as Goliath fell.

A STONE'S THROW

The Israelites feared the Philistines' wrath;
A giant named Goliath stood right in their path.
They basked in confusion with no battle plan,
When one, but a boy, stood up like a man.

He was stricken by fear like all of the rest,
But courageously faced this challenging test.
He brashly proclaimed what it was he would do,
Leaving no choice but to then follow through.

He put on no armor, he carried no sword—
Just a stone and a string and faith in the Lord.
They must have mocked him, laughing out loud.
But David didn't listen to taunts from the crowd.

The giant that stood in the way of success,
Came tumbling down in a minute or less.
When facing a giant, unsure what to do,
Remember how simple the stone David threw.

No matter how hard the success that you seek,
God gave us power through words that we speak.
Your mountain will move from words you say.
Your victory lies just a stone's throw away.

Peter is one of my favorite disciples because he was "out there" and bold about his faith. Unafraid to say what he thought, Peter often got himself into situations. I liked his eagerness to prove his faith and his loyalty.

PETER'S FAITH

As we gazed on the water in the darkness of night,
Something was coming, a small flash of a light.
In the midst of the storm, a shadow came near.
We heard a voice say, "It is I, do not fear."

Peter jumped up and called out His name,
"Jesus, my Lord, let me do the same."
"Step from the boat, Peter, if you believe."
The next thing we saw, we could barely conceive.

Without questions or qualms or hesitancy,
Peter began walking on the waves of the sea.
We had witnessed the miracles that Jesus could do,
But Peter was a man, like me or like you.

Then, as if angry, a thunderous crash,
The storm lit the sky with a lightning bolt flash.
As Peter looked away, the waves pulled him down.
"Save me," he shouted, "I don't want to drown."

Jesus reached in and pulled Peter out.
"How little your faith, Peter, why did you doubt?"
If we step from the boat, if we answer the call,
If we focus on Jesus, He won't let us fall.

EARTHSHAKING FAITH

From the depths of the perilous pit down below,
A strange sort of sound was starting to grow.
The two of them beaten within minutes of death,
The stench of the dungeon, depleting their breath.

It wasn't the moaning that usually occurred.
I couldn't believe what I thought I had heard.
For, there in the darkness, chained to the wood—
Two crazy men singing as loud as they could.

Praises of joy rang out through the halls,
A sound that had never pervaded these walls,
A faith like I never had witnessed before,
Then suddenly, beneath me, a crack in the floor.

The bars on the cells began slowly to shake,
Soon the whole building had started to quake.
The roof began falling, spraying stones all around;
The locks on the doors then all fell to the ground.

The two men kept singing throughout the assault,
Their imminent escape would be rightly my fault.
So, drawing my sword, I was ready to face,
The penalty worthy of such a disgrace.

But, "Wait," I heard, "we all are still here.
Put down your sword and temper your fear."
Their obedience granted them both a release.
Their earthshaking faith had granted them peace.

There are a lot of faith lessons in this story of Paul and Silas.

135

THE LAST SUPPER

He called them together, so much was at stake.
Their last time to gather for bread they could break.
Intently they asked, "Who among us is best?"
He must have considered—could they pass the test?

His ministry relying on a handful of men,
The message of salvation was about to begin.
They had no idea what they'd have to endure.
The lesson He taught them was simple and pure.

He showed by example how a leader must lead;
To serve others first and help those in need.
It's not who's best or who's standing tall,
It's who can best serve the least of them all.

He knew that one day these men would be gone,
Yet the message they carried had to keep living on.
So He taught them to go and be fishers of men.
To go find disciples who would do it again.

By faith, the message would always survive.
Leaders would rise and keep hope alive.
He commissioned their minds to give the world hope
By anointing their feet with water and soap.

The 3:00 shadow is a powerful metaphor. Bible scholars calculate (however they do that) that Jesus died around 3:00. The storm that day must have been incredible.

3:00 SHADOW

The three o'clock shadow that filled up the sky,
A sign from the heavens that few could deny.
The fury of God over what they had done.
The tears of a Father, embracing His Son.

A MOTHER'S SILENCE

If you just can't believe that Jesus was God,
Suspecting conspiracy or well thought out fraud,

When words don't help the truth to come clear,
The silence of Mary is what you should hear.

What Mother would be able to watch her son die,
If she knew deep inside it was really a lie?

Think about it. The silence of Mary speaks volumes to the validity of the crucifixion. What mother could watch her son go through such torture if she knew it was a lie? Would she not have said instead, "Sure, He's crazy; He needs some serious help, but don't crucify Him"?

Chapter 9: Character (Humor)

Character: Honor, truthfulness, personality, trust, faith, loyalty, humor.

"Righteous lips are the delight of kings; and they love him who speaks what is right" (Proverbs 16:13).

What to consider:

- How do your words affect your character?
- Does humor open the door to you sharing your faith?
- What is the difference between "He's a character" and "He's got character"?
- Who are some of the people you've come to count on?

Berry Payton is a good friend who has had several successful business ventures. He uses his humor and insights in an influential way. Character is always forefront in his efforts. It shows in his business, his family, and his life. You never know what to expect from Berry, except that he will do whatever he does with honor, loyalty, and faithfulness.

Berry currently owns and operates a construction company called Payton & Associates based in Bloomington, Indiana. They focus on home restorations and flipping homes with hope to prosper, enjoy the process, and help others along the way.

Guest Foreword by Berry Payton

I have been gainfully self-employed since I was sixteen years old. I have experienced my share of failures. I have also managed to succeed on my own terms. What I've learned through my years of entrepreneurship is: Always remember to retain your character and your sense of humor. It's one thing to have character. It's quite another to be a character.

I have a unique perspective on Kevin. I knew him pre-Marla and pre-Parkinson's. We worked together on a business venture. I watched him come out of his accounting shell and become a dynamic speaker and leader in the business world. Then I saw his creative side come out when he met his beautiful wife, Marla. I also watched him gradually withdraw back into his shell due to the devastation of Parkinson's. Kevin inspires me with his beautiful words through his work and by his life of positive actions and thoughts, overcoming physical challenges and never making excuses. He is a man of character, doing what he is called to do—inspire and challenge others to be the best they can be.

Character is intended to be a noun, but to me it is more of a verb. It's what you do until it becomes who you are. It is not something you can purchase, be awarded, or achieve. It is meticulously and methodically built over time. Building character is a slow process, but can be lost in an instant with a bad decision. When someone has character, it is a measure of being able to trust that person impeccably. Character means different things to different people. It is as hard to define as it is to acquire. Of course, there is only one person who you can totally trust, who has the ultimate "character" and who will never let you down—Jesus.

—Berry Payton

THE SANTA TWIST

One cold Christmas morning, I believe I was eight,
Hook, line, and sinker, I swallowed the bait.
After waking up early, I snuck out to see
What Santa had left for us under the tree.

I recall being shocked as I looked all around.
No presents at all, none to be found.
An impending disaster, how could this be true?
So much for that bike and my roller skates too!

I ran back to bed with tears of despair.
I'm sure I said something like, "Life isn't fair!"
I woke up my sisters and rightly complained—
Santa had skipped us, I sadly explained.

It was certainly their fault, not possibly me.
For I was the **angel** of the family, you see.
I took them to show what damage they'd done,
but it turned out ole Santa was just having fun.

For inside our stockings, a peculiar little note:
"Your first gift is in a place you might float."
The bathtub, I thought, as I raced down the hall
where I found a new glove, a bat, and a ball.

With each gift a clue where the next one would be.
The last one then lead us all back to the tree.
Though it seemed he had filled everything on my list,
Santa had plotted out one final twist.

"Inside is a treasure," was the note Santa signed.
"Always remember, if you seek you will find!"
An old wooden cross that would help us recall
the gift that God gave us, the greatest of all.

We knew in our hearts God's message was true,
but it felt good to know that Santa knew too.

This was one of my favorite childhood memories. Mom (and Santa) managed to orchestrate quite a memorable experience.

As a kid, the youth group leader at my church took me under his wing. He was kind of a loose cannon, doing some crazy things. Mont became a mentor. His faith was strong, his body wasn't. I always looked forward to being around him. He brought a group of diverse kids together who had little in common. He managed to form a tight-knit group who would do many things together. One of Mont's memorable schemes involved displacing the "back row squatters" of our church. I will never forget the looks on their faces. Mont went home to be with Jesus later that year but had created a lasting memory.

THE BACK ROW CONSPIRACY

Such a devious plan we concocted one day,
Kind of mischievous in an ornery way.
The goal was to throw an innocent curve,
Knock people off the routine that they serve.

We showed up early to church that morning,
With no indication, without prior warning.
Some surely thought we had set our clocks wrong.
We'd never shown up before the first song.

The early-to-risers were there hanging out,
No clue what our sinister scheme was about.
We brought doughnuts to share in reception hall,
A diversionary tactic that served as a stall.

It worked to perfection; they didn't even know.
We ran to the sanctuary and filled the back row.
They came in together, the back-row brigade,
Bewildered to discover the prank we had played.

The looks on their faces were priceless to see.
How could this happen? How could this be?
"They've taken our seats," one gruffly replied,
As they shuffled back out to regroup and decide.

We burst out laughing over what we had done,
Then moved up one row after having our fun.
As they sauntered back in, to their cheerful delight,
Somehow the world had again been made right.

Sliding into the row, one leaned up and said,
"Thank you for putting that thought in our head.
We've taken for granted our comfortable place.
God wants us moving and sharing His grace."

Our newfound friends still claim the back pew.
At times we bring doughnuts to see what they'll do.
What started as a joke was a blessing in disguise,
The Sunday we took the back row by surprise.

TWO-MINUTE WARNING

Why do I think of the right thing to say,
Two minutes after my chance goes away?
The perfect retort, laced with some wit,
A brilliant response that shakes them a bit.

A subtle little slam or thought-provoking phrase,
An encouraging word or a Bible verse praise.
If I could cause time to pause for a while,
I could weave my words with precision and style.

But alas, those thoughts don't flow from my head.
They go through some time-delayed process instead.
So if you think I'm too quiet, I need you to stay
Just two minutes longer, so I'll know what to say.

Two-minute warning is so totally me, it is scary. Although it seems, from comments, I am not alone.

A DOPE ON A SLOPE

I must have been crazy but I had been dared;
I couldn't back down or admit I was scared.
My untimely death danced forefront in my mind,
Any thoughts of escape I had left far behind.

A friend said, "It's easy, just glide with the snow.
C'mon, the Black Diamond is where we should go."
With trembling hands, I looked over the crest.
Straight down it appeared as I tightened my vest.

Then somebody nudged me just over the top.
Behind me I heard, "Does he know how to stop?"
I was picking up speed at a dangerous pace,
Like an Olympic contestant in a downhill race.

I screamed, "Hey! Look out! Get out of my way!"
I passed a few friends to their startled dismay.
This must be the end. It was my time to die.
Then I hit an embankment and started to fly.

Falling head over heels in a full double twist,
I landed on my feet and pumped up my fist.
The crowd started cheering my remarkable ride.
I was a little too cocky as I waved in full stride.

With confidence, I thought, that wasn't so tough.
Then some kid whizzed by to show off his stuff.
Now tumbling once again, I barely could see,
The fence I knocked down after grazing that tree.

My buddy plowed in, saying, "Man, are ya dead?
The best way to stop is not with your head."
I tried to jump up, but my skis spun around,
Crossing, then knocking me back to the ground.

The ones who had cheered and thought I was cool,
Now laughed at the perils of this snow-skiing fool.
In the end, I had conquered an enemy I faced:
One ride down the slope, and my fear was erased.

A PIRATE'S QUEST

It was quite an adventure. I never had sailed.
Appearances looked like the last trip had failed.
"That rickety old thing? Ya sure it will float?"
Nodding, my friend said, "Don't call it a boat."

We sat in the back as his dad came up top.
He was dressed like a pirate. I felt my jaw drop.
Wielding a sword, his clothes were so cool.
He was twisting and jabbing as if in a duel.

"What's going on?" I asked with concern.
My buddy said, "Watch, pay attention and learn.
He thinks he's the captain, that this is his ship.
Listen up, or it could be a very long trip."

My eyes were wide open as he tucked in his sword.
This might be a journey I could not afford.
"Arrr! Fresh blood," he said, pointing at me.
"Are ye brave enough, boy, to sail the high sea?"

I cautiously nodded, responding, "Yes, sir!"
He then threw me a coat, why I'm not sure.
He leaped toward the cabin, taking hold of the wheel.
His eye patch and peg leg looked pretty darn real.

"Shiver me timbers and spindle me toes,
Nubs to the wind, which way dar she blows?
You'll swab up them decks and dust off them planks.
Ahoy, ye scoundrels, now scrub out dem tanks."

"Clean out the gallows and hoist up that mast,
I feel a storm brewing. It's coming in fast.
We seek buried treasure, medallions and pearls,
Cast off this island and straighten them curls."

Crashing through waves like butter through steel,
The seduction of danger was casting appeal.
When this incredible journey was finally done,
I said, "Thanks for the ride in your boat. It was fun."

Suddenly the veins in his eyes turned to red.
My friend shook his head, exclaiming, "You're dead."
He wielded his sword like a samurai knight.
I said, "Captain, I don't think you heard me just right.

If you thought I said boat, you misunderstood.
I said, thanks for the coat, it fit me real good."
He then patted my head, put his weapon away.
My friend said, "Nice save, you live one more day."

BE NOT

Be not distracted by trivial things.
Be leery of gifts that promise no strings.

Be careful discerning advice given free.
Be wary of things that come too easily.

Be cautious of others demanding your time.
And be "vewwy afwaid of people who *whyme.*"

THE LIAR'S BENCH

My old hometown has a restaurant where
The older men gather with stories to share.
Many are fabled and some ***almost*** true.
At times I've been known to stretch one or two.

Some craft their words like a lawyer on trial.
But the best are delivered in ***good-ole-boy*** style.
Some doozies, whoppers, and outlandish claims—
Trick is to go just so far that some doubt remains.

How big was that fish? How tough was that shot?
How fast were you going last ticket you got?
How hard did you have it? How bad could it be?
There's always one better, just wait and you'll see.

With memories embellished, a sight to behold.
Legends are born from stories they've told.
They'll say what they think if you give one a try.
There's plenty of coffee. It helps if you buy.

I've saved up a few that I can't wait to tell,
From that old corner booth I remember so well.
So if you're ever in town, come by and we'll stop
By the Liar's Bench over at Joe's Coffee Shop.

This one is about my grandpa, Lamar Gardner, and the Ellettsville (Indiana) Village Inn where he used to hang out. Every small town has one; go hang out there for a while, you might find a story or two.

WHO'S GONNA PAY?

This rhyme is a riddle. The answer you'll find
If you listen intently, with a clutter-free mind.
It's something you pay but never with cash,
Can arrive in an instant or be gone in a flash.

It won't cost you much unless you don't pay.
What a difference it makes if done the right way.
It's not found in stores, displayed on the racks.
There's no recognition through ribbons or plaques.

If you choose not to pay, it could cost a lot.
If you don't pay enough, someday you'll get caught.
It's available at prices everyone can afford.
If you don't pay at all, you may become bored.

If you do pay in full, you'll find what it takes,
But anything short of that costs you mistakes.
If you strive for success, you'll consistently pay.
If you typically don't, you'll be in the way.

There are so many things that this can enhance—
Your family, career, maybe even romance.
It deftly determines how far you will go;
If you're doing it now then you already know.

If you still need a clue after reading this rhyme,
Try it once more, pay the answer this time.

THE ANSWER:
You must give it your all. You can't merely try.
If you don't ***pay attention***, life passes you by!

THEORY INFRACTION

When flashing red lights engulfed my rear view,
I actually cussed, which I rarely will do.
Hastened to consider my excuse rather quick,
I needed a story to make this not stick.

"Good morning, officer," in an innocent way.
He asked was I "in a big hurry today?"
I rambled some nonsense on writing a book.
But I saw that familiar raised-eyebrow look.

That's when these words began spilling out;
I said, "I've a theory, here's what it's about;
It seems the whole world can be slowed down by one
Inconsiderate person, simply driving for fun.

If they caused a doctor a ten-minute delay,
Then ten with appointments become late that day.
Those ten might then pass on ten minutes each,
To ten other people whom they were to reach.

A hundred now affected by one driver's hands.
Are you starting to see how this theory expands?
So I thought to myself, if this theory were true,
I should speed up—as a courtesy to you.

I was merely attempting to do something great,
Enabling those following me not to be late."
With a stoic reply, he exclaimed, "That makes sense.
I completely understood your logical defense."

I asked for a warning instead of a fine.
He shook his head, "No, not after that line.
The reason is simple, my shift ends at four.
My wife hangs a honey-do list on the door.

If I could delay her ten minutes I'd find
A chance to relax, a chance to unwind.
According to your theory, that's easy to do.
Just slow someone down; I'm starting with you!"

HUMOROUS SAYINGS

Try to keep up or you're likely to find
You'll get tired of chasing someone's behind.

God loves us so much that He counts every hair,
It just doesn't take long when nothing is there.

There are those who go far, but not very straight.
There are those who go slow, and those who can't wait.
In the fairways of life, if you want to survive,
Learn to yell, "Fore!" I've seen how you drive.

Remember how simple life was 'til we bought
All the make-your-life-simple contraptions we've got?

You want to stand out, but no one can tell?
Learn how to pray if you want to rebel.

Why would God bless us if all that we do
Is show up on Sundays and park in the pew?

If your goal is to live in a castle someday,
There may be some dragons you'll first have to slay.

At times I am puzzled which way I should go,
Until it is clear that I really don't know.

Just when I thought things couldn't get worse,
I caught the affliction of writing in verse.

Note to myself: not to write anymore
Notes 'til I've read all the ones from before.

If you're honest in all the statements you've made.
You won't have to cover the tracks you have laid.

To get what you want, it's a matter of style,
Just flash them that big irresistible smile.

Chapter 10: Hope (Parkinson's)

Hope: Promise, expectation, belief, faith.

"Be of good courage, and He shall strengthen your
heart, all you who hope in the Lord" (Psalms 31:24).

What to consider:

- What or who do you find hope in?
- What does it mean to "hope in the Lord"? Have you ever lost hope?
- Do you hope your faith is true, or do you believe that it is?

Don Waterman is one of the most humble human beings I know. He is a fellow Parkinson's sufferer. A farmer at heart, he has the unique ability to see the *simple* in things. When he was diagnosed, his family rallied around him and started the Indiana Parkinson Foundation, which helps people affected by PD reclaim their lives. Don has passionately and relentlessly served the Parkinson's community. Always putting others before himself, he has raised the hopes of many who were facing a hopeless situation.

Check out www.indianaparkinsonfoundation.org for Don and his family's incredible story.

Guest Foreword by Don Waterman

I am a person most undeserving of the recognition that I have received. My family deserves the thanks for those who have found hope in the midst of despair. I am grateful for the opportunity to serve others. Before Parkinson's, I remember questioning my significance in life. Now I have found it: to show God's love and hope to as many people affected by Parkinson's as I can. I despise this disease, but God has shown me that though we may suffer, He is the source of our hope. I know as I finish this race, I will see Him face to face.

I have been a farmer all my life. I have witnessed the miracle of new life as seed is placed in the ground. I have seen the magical look on a child's face as she holds a new yellow chick. I've seen that seed produce a yield of a hundredfold, and the chick grow to become a hen that lays eggs. I don't think there is a better place on earth to witness hope than on a farm. As a farmer, all I could do was prepare the soil, put the seed in it, try to keep the weeds out, and hope for a harvest. I could not make it grow. I learned early on that I was not in control. That is where *hope* comes in. The best words to describe hope are trust and expectation. Hope is much the way our exercise class called The Climb works. If you come hoping to improve your quality of life but do not participate, your hope fades. Hope involves energy and input on your part.

Kevin and Marla are two amazing people I have met through Parkinson's disease. They love the Lord and are as dedicated to serving the Parkinson community as I am. They serve on our Board of Directors of the Indiana Parkinson Foundation, and Marla from time to time is masterful at putting me in my place. I love you both and *hope* this book is a best seller.

— Don Waterman

PARKINSON'S: A Life Sentence or a Sentence for Life?

It started when the little finger on my left hand stopped wanting to type. My third finger was taking over. When I got really cold, my left shoulder shook. I also noticed that my left arm didn't swing like my right one. There were occasions when I tried to throw a baseball and it wouldn't come out of my fingers correctly. One other early symptom (that I barely noticed) was losing my sense of smell. I went to my doctor and he said it was probably nothing. Then a year later when the symptoms hadn't gone away, he suggested I see a neurologist. I barely knew what Parkinson's was until my neurologist said he thought I had it.

My reaction, because I was much too busy to be that inconvenienced, was to just ignore it. My denial lasted for several years, until symptoms started to become noticeable to other people. I had learned to hide it well. Aside from the obvious physical shortcomings Parkinson's brings, the non-physical are perhaps worse. I started withdrawing from personal interactions. Rather than meeting with people I did everything through e-mail or over the phone. I did whatever I could to avoid controversy and confrontations because my body would start to shake. It does get a little better when you start to tell people about your disease instead of trying so hard to conceal it. I often kept my hand in my pocket or learned how to position my arm on my hip to keep from shaking. I often thought others imagined I was nervous. The mental aspect of PD can be as paralyzing as the physical.

The financial side of Parkinson's can also be devastating. Obviously the medical and pharmacy bills can add up, but there are other, more subtle factors. I was stuck in a position in which the best way for me to progress in my career was to take a controller job at another facility. However, my diagnosis prevented me from being a suitable candidate. I stayed ten-plus years in a position for which I was overqualified. People might think they are covered for this kind of devastation because they have a "disability policy." Most disability policies only cover 60 percent of your income, and even less than that when they don't consider vacations or bonuses as income. Then I had to have health insurance. Welcome to

COBRA, which cost over $500 per month (as opposed to the $50/month I was paying). Then my unscrupulous insurance company (whom I can't even mention by name) stopped my benefits for four years because they claimed I had been overpaid. Around $15,000 in legal fees later, and their team of lawyers forced me into taking a settlement far less than what I was owed. I was out of resources and they knew it. Pile on top of all that pharmaceutical prescriptions that were close to our house payment each month. Suffice it to say, Parkinson's can be devastating in more ways than one.

I know this all sounds like I am frustrated. I am not. I may have a slightly unhealthy disdain for crooked lawyers, but I look on my life with Parkinson's as a blessing. I am now twenty-five years into my Parkinson's journey. Looking back, I wonder where I would have been without it. Likely stuck in an office somewhere, working sixty hours per week, engulfed in what "the world" has to offer. I spent the first ten years praying for God to cure me of this dreadful disease. Then it occurred to me that Parkinson's might be my "cure." Without it I might never have had the time to come close to God. Not that God gave it to me, but He sure made it work for me. Everyone has something they deal with; I am no different. I tell you these things not for sympathy, but merely to share my experience with others.

Deep Brain Stimulation

In 2011, twenty years into my journey, I had a brain surgery called DBS (Deep Brain Stimulation). I was diagnosed about the same time (and we are the same age) as Michael J. Fox. Michael had the procedure done relatively early in his journey with limited success (from what I understand). Mine, however, was a huge success. I was fortunate that my symptoms began on my left side (I'm right-handed), and tremors were never a dominant symptom. The problem I had was different—to be able to move I had to take a healthy amount of medicine. Then when the medicine kicked in, it would be too much for me, and I experienced anxiety and involuntary jerky movements called dyskinesia. It's funny—I've had many people over the years claim they could *cure my perils* with their unique product. My response was, "I can cure it! I could stop taking medicine, but then I won't be able to move at all."

DBS involves two wires that go deep into the brain and an electric stimulator box in the chest that sends a constant signal. I won't even pretend to know how it works. When the signal is adjusted correctly, it acts like you've just taken medicine. Most people can reduce their medicine intake by fifty percent or more. I have had a 95-100 percent reduction in my medicine. When I share with people, especially fellow "Parkies," that I have endured twenty-five years and am on no meds, they are amazed. It's not that I am symptom free. DBS doesn't work on everything. My balance is off, my sense of smell is gone, my voice has become so soft people barely hear me. My handwriting is illegible, and I have trouble articulating the words that I put together in my head. It has all happened gradually. Most friends and family think I'm just quiet and don't talk much. They don't know or see the "me" trapped inside, the *me* that could have been. DBS has allowed me the little things (what seems little to most) like going through the day almost forgetting I have PD. Prior to surgery, there was a 24/7 reminder that something was terribly wrong. I can walk in crowds now without worrying about freezing in place right in front of someone. We can leave with everyone else when a movie is over. We used to wait until everyone else was gone because I didn't want to walk ahead of them. The downfall is I have to go in every four years for an outpatient surgery to change my battery.

Exercise is vitally important for Parkinson's patients. We are a part of a wonderful program with the Indiana Parkinson Foundation (IPF) called The Climb. It is an exercise program specifically targeted for improving the lives of Parkinson's patients. IPF is a wonderful community where we have made many friends. We proudly serve on the board of directors and help out as much as we can.

All is good with our family. Marla and I have a great loving relationship. We spend almost all our time together and love it that way. We have learned through our struggles to live below our means and to faithfully, and joyfully, tithe without question. God can do more with ninety percent of our income than we can with a hundred. We have made hundreds of friends through our interactions. Life is blessed beyond measure. Our hope for you, no matter what you may be going through, is peace, the kind of peace that passes all understanding. The peace that only God, the Father can supply.

LIFE IS NOT FAIR

"Life is not fair," we emphatically explain.
Why is there suffering, heartache, and pain?
With burdens to carry and crosses to bear,
Sometimes we wonder, does God even care?

While many face trials beyond what we could,
Some receive more than it seems like they should.
Life is not fair. It's a burdensome task,
Begging the question that most will not ask.

If God made life fair, would we all be the same?
Would we all dress alike and have the same name?
Would our joys be sweet, our victories strong?
Could we even decide between right and wrong?

Would we have thrilling highs or challenging lows,
Struggles to overcome or life-changing blows?
Would victories cease because someone would lose?
Might chances exist for things we could choose?

If ambition and courage became obsolete,
Could we set any goals we'd strive to complete?
Would heaven's gate open for all to come in?
It wouldn't be fair to be banned just for sin.

Should God grant our wish, I believe we'd declare,
"Something's not right about life being fair."

When that old line arises, give them this thought,
"You're exactly right. Thank God that it's not!"

My grandfather, Lamar Gardner, was a reluctant farmer in Iowa. Reluctant in that he never really wanted to be a farmer, but health situations with his father forced him into it. He was always the one neighboring farmers came to in need. He would have made a great mechanical engineer. Sadly, I did not inherit any of his carpentry or mechanical skills. I like to think I inherited some of his ingenuity though. It wasn't until after he died that I found out he wrote poetry in his younger days. He was a typical farmer, set in his ways (which was, of course, the only way). He had his hard side, but as a grandchild I got to see some of his softer side as well. I wrote this as a tribute to him. He didn't really say any of these things, but he showed them. Thanks, Grandpa!

A FARMER BY TRADE

A farmer by trade, he worked on the land.
He understood things that few understand.

When plowing the fields, his mind would be filled
With lessons in life he taught and instilled.
"Life's pretty simple," my grandpa would claim.
"The rules we should live by are always the same."
He delivered his thoughts in a wry kind of style.
You'd think he was mad, but then he would smile.

He was always profound, a man of his word.
He always looked forward, despite what occurred.
"I've never reaped anything I didn't first sow.
The seed that you plant is the crop that will grow.
Fix your eyes on a spot, if you want to plow straight.
If you need to start over, it's never too late."

One thing I remember, he often would share,
"Don't tear down a fence 'til you know why it's there.
Some fences are built to keep danger away;
Some fences are built so we'll know where to stay."
His philosophy in life was, "Let people be.
I'm not here to judge, lest they should judge me."

"Some things are better off left on the ground;
Manure doesn't stink 'til you stir it around."
The best thing he taught me was how I could find
The answer to anything crossing my mind.
Whatever I'd ask him, he'd get out the Book,
Saying, "God wrote it down, if you take time to look."

He worked on the land, a farmer by trade.
He never will know the impact he made.

MAJESTIC PERFECTION

Standing with grace, alone in a field,
The essence of valor, God's glory revealed;
A stark silhouette through storm-scattered skies,
A ray of hope drenched in a gorgeous sunrise.

Eloquently crafted for the world to behold,
Like a solitary soldier, so masterfully bold.
With arms outstretched, uniquely designed,
Peaceful, pristine, exactly aligned.

Patiently waiting to bud in the spring,
Another year past, another trunk ring.
The morning mist painting a canvas reflection,
A perfect tree cast in majestic perfection.

FREE ADVICE

Why do we listen to those with no clue,
As if they would know what it is we should do?
Their convincing opinions are often delivered,
On things they have barely even ever considered.

Speaking with confidence, they'll boldly proclaim
What they have experienced was "almost the same."
As if there should be no question or doubt,
When they don't even know what they're talking about.

Why ask them, "How?" on things they've not done,
Things they've not finished or even begun?
They don't really care, they just want to vent.
Free advice often is worth what you spent.

Wouldn't you rather seek opinions from those
Who've already succeeded at what you propose?
You don't ask a lawyer what medicine you need.
Why ask someone failing, "How do I succeed?"

If you're being astute, then you'll possibly claim
The advice in this message is free just the same.
So, out of concern, not wanting you to fail,
I've decided to charge you; my bill's in the mail.

Remember that magical look of surprise
When looking at life through childlike eyes?

DARE TO BE GREAT

You're writing the script. You're playing the scene.
You carry a vision that no one has seen.
It's a chance to embrace the arms of fate.
Will you let it pass by or dare to be great?

One person can make a difference, it's true.
Despite sounding crazy, why can't it be you?
If you give it to God, your dream will survive.
The words that you speak will bring it alive.

If you continue to give all the glory to Him,
Your cup will be filled, overflowing the brim.
A door has swung open that may quickly shut:
A way to escape your monotonous rut.

It's right in your grasp if you'll simply hold on.
Enjoy every moment 'til the journey is gone.
Chase it right now or you'll always question why
You didn't take the chance, or didn't even try.

God will provide everything that you need.
Faith will determine where your calling will lead.
You are the one! God is counting on you!
The challenge is here, now what will you do?

If God had a fridge, guess who'd be there?
You in the middle of a big white-edged square.

GONE TO THE DOGS

I was riding the bumper of an old pickup truck.
Running late for a meeting—that's my kind of luck.
With no chance to pass on a thin curvy road,
I pounded the wheel, just about to explode.
An old country farmer simply out for a ride,
Two sheep in the back and a dog by his side.

Forced into a pace I considered too slow,
I watched as his dog put on quite a show.
As though the first time he'd ridden before,
Or last and would not get to ride anymore.
His excitement was quite intriguing to me.
He stretched out his head like a captain at sea.

He hung out so far, holding on with his paws,
His ears flapped behind in constant applause.
His tongue, hanging out like a Jordanesque move,
With nothing held back and nothing to prove.
He bounced back and forth, giving each side a try,
When I noticed a chance to pass passed me by.

This dog was enthused about being alive,
While I had been struggling to merely survive.
So I stuck out my head as far as I could:
The wind in my face; he was right, it felt good.
If anyone watched, I'm sure it looked strange.
It was nice to enjoy letting loose for a change.

I learned a great lesson from that old gray hound.
The world is amazing if you just look around.
As things turned out it was a very lucky day,
Except for the bug I swallowed on the way.

Chapter 11: Wisdom (Life Lessons)

Wisdom: Knowledge, prudence, discernment, trust, life lessons, ingenuity, knack.

"If any of you lacks wisdom, let him ask of God, who gives to all liberally and without reproach, and it will be given to him" (James 1:5).

What to consider:

- Are you watching for life's little lessons along the way? Sometimes the hardest answers come in the simplest ways.
- How do you gain wisdom in your life?

Tim Burton is one of the greatest leaders I know. After having already been successful in the business world, he and his wife Angie decided to tap a maple tree on his farm. This ingenuity led to his adventure into the maple syrup world. *Burton's Maplewood Syrup Farm* has an awesome following. Tim got the idea of infusing the flavor of his maple syrup with the flavor remnants from whiskey and bourbon barrels. This sensational idea and the ability to brand it has created a maple syrup phenomenon. He has marketed his syrup to chefs around the world. Tim, never lacking for words, can be found spreading the news of his fantastic story, his amazing syrup, and his Smile Foundation, raising funds to help children with facial anomalies.

You can read their story and order their syrup by visiting: www.burtonsmaplewoodfarm.com.

Guest Foreword by Tim Burton

People ask me all the time, "Are you the real Tim Burton?" Guess that depends on your perspective—whether you're a Johnny Depp fan or a maple syrup lover. Either way, yes I am real. I was born Timothy P. Burton. So, I guess perspective is everything, which brings me to my perspective of the wisdom of my good friend, Kevin Pace. I had the pleasure of meeting Kevin when he was assistant controller at Bloomington Hospital. From the first time we met, Kevin struck me as a well-balanced, even-keeled, thinking kind of guy. Though his life's lens wasn't always rosy, he always looked at life in a positive way. What I've learned from Kevin is that adversity doesn't build character—it reveals it. Because of that, my perspective in and of life has been forever changed, and I've become a bit wiser man.

People told me I was crazy to start a maple syrup farm on our property in tiny Medora, Indiana. I had a lot to learn. Wisdom is the application of knowledge. If you don't apply your knowledge, nothing ever comes of it. When I look at a maple tree, it is full of knowledge, brimming with potential. If you never "tap" into that potential, you never discover the awesome flavor it has to share from deep within. We call it "God's candy." It takes ingenuity and work for knowledge to become wisdom. It takes true wisdom to create success in this life. Knowledge is knowing that Jesus is Lord. Even Satan has this kind of knowledge. It's what you do with it that's important. Wisdom, however, is making the decision to make Jesus Christ Lord of your life.

—Tim Burton

THE SCAR

The scar that goes with you wherever you go—
The mark of a struggle most people don't know.
A badge you must wear and carry around
From battles you've fought on spiritual ground.

Its presence reminds you of a much harder day.
You'll make it, no matter what stands in your way.
You are a survivor! You've done it before.
Satan carries no power over you anymore.

He's taken his shots; you're still standing strong.
You laughed in his face and yelled, "Move along!"
The wound is now healed, a scar in its place—
Strength you can draw for challenges you face.

As it quietly fades a little more every day,
You wish it were gone, yet hope it would stay.
The symbol of a journey not chosen to take,
A reminder God's love will never forsake.

Everything works when the timing is right;
Even the battle won't seem like a fight.

At the crack of dawn, the rooster crows,
The bacon fries, and the coffee flows.
A constant reminder, a daily alarm.
Time to give thanks for a day on the farm.

A GOD-AWESOME DAY

It happened each morning the very same way.
"Rise up, young man, it's gonna be a great day!"
I remember a time, with a goal to sleep late,
I questioned her why this day would be great.
She said, "It's a choice that we each must decide:
Embrace God's gift or pull the covers and hide."

"Then if I can choose, not trying to be mean,
I don't like this annoying great-day routine."
My response took her back. She thought for a bit,
Then softly replied, "If you want, then I'll quit."
My last wake-up call had finally been cast,
Though it wasn't her nature to give in so fast.

I'd managed to escape some childish traditions;
Independence, I reasoned, from useless renditions.
The next several mornings seemed sort of strange:
Just a knock on my door and a simple exchange.
It didn't take long, a couple of bad days,
I soon began missing that miserable phrase.

Something was different, my life out of place.
As if I were running just slightly off pace.
The reason she did it, I finally knew,
To teach me the power of words we construe.
I was much too stubborn to admit my mistake,
But knew in my heart, amends I should make.

The next time she knocked, I was ready to say,
"Thanks, Mom! Today is a **God-Awesome** day!"
She opened the door and smiled back inside.
"Yes, son, it is, if that's what you decide."

AN OLD FRIEND

The scars that it shows from storms it has fought
Show character, history, and maybe some rot.
The chains have all rusted. It sways just a bit.
It's not the most comfortable place you could sit.

It creaks and it cracks whenever it swings.
The stains are still there from Coke bottle rings.
It holds the reflection of memories faint,
Cascading somewhere between layers of paint.

The grains in the wood like stones in a brook,
A heritage written like pages in a book.
Imagine the stories this friend must have heard:
Someone to listen without saying a word.

A part of the family, these boards have become,
An acquaintance to many, a best friend to some.
Graciously capturing the joys we have shared,
Softening tears in times we've despaired.

Where problems were solved, lives turned around,
Where lessons were posed, answers were found,
Where dreams were born on clear starry nights,
Where refuge was taken from long drawn-out fights.

The hope is this swing will stay in its place,
And help those to come in things they will face.
A prayer that this swing, which embraces their past,
Keeps them from living their lives way too fast.

A TIME-SAVING IDEA

Time has a way of controlling our thoughts.
Our days quickly pass like calendar-dots.
We search for conveniences, easier ways;
We try to cut corners to lengthen our days.
In attempts to do all this life has to give,
We use the old adage, "We've one life to live."

Yet, somehow it goes, the more things we try,
The faster life seems to be passing us by.
If we could buy back all the time we have lost
On time-saving gadgets that lower our cost,
We might understand there is no time to waste
On things that won't last, garnered in haste.

THE WALL

The wall we've constructed, protecting our pride,
Brings safety and refuge, a place we can hide.
It holds off our enemies, challengers, and foes.
The greater the threat, the higher it goes.
But the wall doesn't care to whom it defends;
It also keeps out our family and friends.

The goal is before you, the task is at hand.
Mountains will move as you so command.
With courage and faith, conviction and pride,
Nothing can stop you with God on your side.

PROPORTIONAL LOGIC

Sometimes my prayers leave me questioning why
It seems God ignores me and doesn't reply.
Then, I think, maybe…the reason could be
He's responding the same way He's treated by me.

I don't always ask Him the things that I should,
I don't keep on praying when everything's good.
I expect God, it seems, to handle my needs,
Cater to incessant ranting and pleads.

Yet, what am I willing to give in return?
I'm sorry! Excuses, complaints, and concerns.
Why would He answer or bless me at all,
When I seem so unwilling to answer His call?

SOME SEE

Some see the doughnut, others see the hole.
Some see the chance, others see the toll.
Some will prepare before they begin,
Others will play with the hope they can win.

Some count their blessings when things are tight;
Others only talk of how nothing goes right.
Some see the struggle as a way to improve;
Others get stuck in a place they can't move.

A PLACE TO CALL HOME

The home in my head has solid oak doors,
Impressive stone walls, and red parquet floors.
There's a warm cozy room you are welcome to see,
But anything beyond that requires a key.

The home in my head I work on each day,
With some things I hide, some I display.
Each room decorated by hopeful ambitions,
Memorable events and cherished traditions.

The home in my head is architecturally sound,
Molded and crafted by treasures I've found.
The foundation is built with illustrious dreams,
Securely supported by hand-chiseled beams.

The home in my head, the place I retreat,
Where victories outweigh any thoughts of defeat,
Where memories are kept and often replayed,
Creations are born and journeys are made.

The home in my head, with treasures I hold,
Moments recalled, and stories once told,
Cascading with pictures of family and friends,
Filling the hallways, corridors, and bends.

The home in my head, this heaven I've built,
A lifelong collection woven in quilt.
The words on the door from a book I have read:
Come rest, weary soul, in the home in my head.

KEEP THE CHANGE

We desperately cling to the things that we know.
When faced with a change, we don't want to go.
We embrace the familiar like a long-lost friend,
  Scared of the wind as our tree starts to bend.

We accept something old but run from the new.
Each Sunday we sit in the same old church pew.
We seek to find structure, a routine we can set;
  We're leery of anything we haven't tried yet.

We talk to the people we've talked to before.
We tend to leave closed, opportunity's door.
Finding safety in things we've previously cast,
  We limit our future by measuring our past.

Old patterns run deep, as we're tempted to stay,
In the same place, doing the same thing every day,
The same TV shows, the same time each week.
Forgotten are goals that we once strove to seek.

We get so entrenched and set in our way,
  Successfully molding the rut where we stay.
Our schedule is full. There's no time it seems,
To even consider those old childhood dreams.

It's simply a choice that we choose to make.
A willing accomplice on the path we take.
But forming new habits against those we've laid,
  Would be a big change of which we're afraid.

UNTHINKABLE FATES

I vividly remember the moment it occurred.
My mind can recite each particular word.
We were hanging around by the locker room door,
To congratulate the team for winning once more.

It was a tournament game with a large rowdy crowd.
The fans had been cheering especially loud.
Caught up in excitement for a moment or two,
I reveled in victory with friends whom I knew.

Then suddenly I realized my hands dangled free.
He was no longer there, anywhere I could see.
I looked all around and called out his name.
I sternly demanded, "Stop playing this game!"

I searched through the building, raced down the hall.
I heard no response to my heart-wrenching call.
I ran through the gym, then out past the gates.
I fought off the fears of unthinkable fates.

Panic ensued as I questioned everyone.
"Have you seen my boy? Have you seen my son?"
I tried to hold back but the thought entered in,
What if I never get to see him again?

My anguish was causing my body to shake,
As thoughts turned to desperate measures to take.
A feeling I'd never confronted before,
I fell to my knees, right there on the floor.

I yelled out, "God, please, don't take him away!"
Tears filled my eyes as I knelt there to pray.
That's when I saw him come running down the hall.
Every possible emotion, I'd been through them all.

An answer to prayer on his jubilant face.
He jumped in my arms, a welcomed embrace!
"Dad, what's the matter? I said I'd be back.
Grandpa was showing me his new Cadillac."

I still don't remember him telling me that,
But I'll never forget what I had to combat.
The thing that I learned from facing my fear
Was don't take for granted he'll always be here.

Based on a true experience, "Unthinkable Fates" tries to describe the horrible, helpless feeling of not knowing where your child was.

WHEN LIFE DRAWS A LINE

A choice is presented, when life draws a line.
Is it masking temptation, or truly divine?
Does it show the way forward, or just set us back?
Will it take us in circles, or keep us on track?

Would it change the direction we're currently on?
What if it's here for a moment, then gone?
Could this be our chance to finally shine?
Is it some kind of calling, or signal, or sign?

Why can't it be marked, like a page in a book?
How will we know if we don't really look?
If we're faithful and willing, then God will design,
The perfect solution, when life draws a line.

Words matter in how parents raise children. We often unknowingly program things into them. The words we speak are incredibly powerful creative tools. If a child has challenges in a certain area, speak potential into them by telling them over and over how good they are at it. Kids hear how you introduce them to others and exactly what you say about them. You have the ability to speak into them the behavior that you want. I was always the "shy" one growing up. But I'm not really that way, I just listen more than I talk. If your child tends to be messy, start praising them in front of others about how cleanly they are. Then sit back and watch the magic happen. The thing is though, it is not magic. It is a biblical principle that works whether you believe it or not. "Programmed That Way" is a true story that happened at one of our shows. This parent was unintentionally enforcing the exact behavior she was trying to remove from her child.

PROGRAMMED THAT WAY

I wanted to shake her, a child was at stake.
She was making a common universal mistake.
"This is my son," she introduced him that day.
"He's terribly shy," as the boy turned away.

Her attempts at explaining the way he behaved,
Were just reinforcing the words she enslaved.
The easy thing would have been simply agree,
Not risking the anger she might feel toward me.

But, I knelt down and looked that boy in the eyes.
"Let me tell you a story that you might recognize.
It's about a young boy who listened quite well.
He learned from the things that people would tell.

Everyone told him he was terribly shy,
So that's what he thought, without questioning why.
Then one day a preacher, courageous and strong,
Informed him that what he'd been told was all wrong.

'You're the child of a King, a miracle of God.
On the day you were born, angels stood to applaud.
People should learn from the gift you possess,
To listen a lot more, and to talk a bit less.'"

THE WAITING GAME

We believe that God has a purpose in mind,
A thing we must do, a path we must find.
We struggle and search, we listen for clues.
We battle distractions that only confuse.

We pray for discernment, a crystal-clear sign.
We're willing to follow God's sovereign design.
He's given us talents, insights, and skills.
We seek to do things that our calling fulfills.

But maybe His blessings are held back for when
We *choose* what we want and not until then.
If our kids would ask us what they should pursue,
We'd pledge our support in whatever they do.

Yet, we wonder why God has yet to provide,
When maybe, He's waiting for us to decide.

WISDOM SAYINGS

That which will make you stand out in a crowd
Is taking a stand, for which you are proud.

Giving your word is like drawing a line.
Keeping your word is a character sign.

Fighting through all those continuous blows
Prepares you for when opportunity shows.

Character reflects in whatever you do;
You never know when there are eyes upon you.

When scarred by lines of shattered dreams,
When hope is all gone, or at least so it seems,
A dreamer at heart will discover a way
To rise up and bloom again the next day.

Despite any bruises from battles we've fought,
We will stick together, no matter what spot.

The illusion of boundaries we build in our mind
Keeps us from finding the thing we must find.

It's often the case that hope is inspired
At times we are broken, exhausted, and tired.

There are moments when all you can do is applaud
At the awesome, magnificent glory of God.

Your life is a story; the world is your stage.
Write with conviction each passionate page.

When one tiny drip makes one tiny drop,
The impact it makes won't easily stop.

Be ever aware of the shadow you cast;
The impression you make will indelibly last.

The poison of pride can cause you to fall;
The passion of pride will make you stand tall.

Remember to always say, "Thank you and please."
The answers you seek you will find on your knees.

If you plan to succeed, the thing you must do
Is plan to succeed and then follow through.

It's hard to help others when the thing they most need
Is the thing you don't have unless you succeed.

I tried hard to prove to God that I can,
But I proved it was better to follow His plan.

Half-full or half-empty the argument goes:
Whatever the answer, your attitude shows.
Another conclusion that most do not see
Is a glass twice as big as really needs be.

Most of our memories eventually fade,
Except for the ones we've intentionally made.

Though storms distract you and things may go wrong,
Don't weary in well-doing. Stay focused, stay strong.

When they said I was crazy, that's when I knew
I was doing exactly what it is I should do.

Hope is contagious, belief is the seed.
Follow someone who knows how to succeed.

Remember that you are the one in control.
Keep your eyes focused and fixed on the goal.

Rather than whine about what you deserve,
If you want to be blessed, learn how to serve.

Count up your blessings with every defeat;
Know that the struggle makes victory sweet.

No matter how hard you get knocked to the floor,
Praise God for the pruning and come back for more.

Wouldn't you rather seek opinions from those
Who've already succeeded at what you propose?

Magnificent to behold in the eyes of a dreamer,
A treasure to be sold in the eyes of a schemer.

If we stick with the basics that keep us on track,
We won't get caught saying, "We've got to go back."

The seduction of evil is beautifully spun;
The trap has been set, the game has begun.
Be wary of things too good to be true,
The web of destruction can hold you like glue.

From the depths of despair, champions will rise
At the point when they face what seems certain demise.

If we all pooled our problems, then drew from a sack,
We'd likely discover we'd want our own back.

Somehow it goes, the more things we try,
The faster life seems to be passing us by.

The chance to soar to incredible heights
Comes from pursuing those "maybes" and "mights."

When destiny's call is clearly in view,
You'll instinctively know what it is you must do.

The demons around you have one common goal:
To make your goal common, distracting your soul.

If we can look back and proudly proclaim
With dignity and honor we've glorified His name,
Then rest in assurance, His grace will abide;
Our nation will prosper with God on our side.

We honor the lives of those who have died
To bring us the freedom that once was denied.

A symbol, our nation proudly adores
The magnificent beauty of an eagle that soars.

When you speak words of honor, character shows.
When you honor your words, character grows.

A masterpiece painted with artistic flair,
The sky is a canvas where angels can share.

No matter how ragged, no matter how torn,
Old Glory reminds us of where we were born.

Some see the struggle, some see the dance.
Some see the challenge, some see the chance.
Some see the forest, some see the trees.
Some see the beauty that no one else sees.

A house is constructed with hammer and nails;
A home is established when family prevails.
A heritage is built through trials we face.
A legacy is born from beliefs we embrace.

If you want them to somehow remember your name,
Listen intently, and do just the same.

We tend toward the edges, we run the fence line.
We test all the boundaries that limits define.
Despite all our questions, the answer we lack—
Does the fence keep us in or hold something back?

The anguish that causes a willow to weep
Is also the reason its roots run so deep.

In the river of life, there are many canoes.
We don't often get the one we would choose.
At times we're too focused on what we have not,
Forgetting to paddle the one that we've got.

If you're willing to listen, commitment grows.
If you're willing to stand, conviction shows.
If you're willing to learn, courage defines.
If you're willing to teach, character shines.

A thousand-step journey, you'll never get done,
Or one simple step, a thousand times one?

To dance face to face, to dance toe to toe,
To dance with a passion that few people know.
To dance with a purpose, leaving nothing to chance,
To follow your calling, for life is to dance.

When someone does nothing, no one prevails.
When no one does anything, everyone fails.
When someone does everything, no one begins.
When everyone does something, everyone wins.

You may think the price of success is too high,
The effort too great for you even to try,
But the true cost of failing can easily exceed
The price you will pay when you choose to succeed.

You can worry and stress over what you have not,
Or cherish the beauty of what you have got.
One makes you measure the price you have spent,
The other brings peace that will make you content.

By teaching the leaders of tomorrow today,
By showing them how they can make their own way,
When tomorrow arrives, we won't have to say
Things aren't as good as they were yesterday.

A friend stands behind you when no one else might.
A good friend stands by you through battles you fight.
A close friend stands with you when things aren't so good.
A best friend stands for you when no one else would.

Chapter 12: Faith

Faith: Belief, hope, courage, strength, conviction, honor, loyalty.

"But without faith it is impossible to please Him, for he who comes to God must believe that He is, and that he is a rewarder of those who diligently seek Him" (Hebrews 11:6).

What to consider:

- What are the outward signs that Christ is alive in your life?
- Often, we get exactly what we speak. Why is that?
- How does your faith react when faced with a challenge?

Russ Abel is the senior pastor at the St. Joseph United Methodist Church in Fort Wayne, Indiana. Russ was a high school friend. He was the kind of kid you'd never believe would become a pastor, but he was always passionate about whatever he did. He now uses his tremendous faith and experience to lead his prospering church in a great way.

You can visit his church at www.stjoemin.com.

Guest Foreword by Pastor Russ Abel

"Now faith is the substance of things hoped for, the evidence of things not seen" (Hebrews 11:1).

For so long I misunderstood faith. I thought faith was the way we made sure bad things were lessened, pain was minimized, and life was made *good.* I looked for a faith that would allow me to *skate* through life. But then, in the midst of my pursuit of such a faith, really bad things happened around me. I realized that faith was so much more than I thought.

Faith is the way God guides and accompanies us through the challenges life brings. It is not an escape; it is not a way to avoid; it is not a divine insurance policy. No, it is so much more than that. Faith becomes the way we live, and even thrive, in spite of the challenges we face. Faith moves us from what is seen to what is unseen, and in so doing our capacity to overcome increases. Rather than being a bridge between good moments of life, faith is, in fact, the constant hope of God in our lives. Not a bridge, but a road upon which we travel.

As you read the following pages, I encourage you to open yourself to the words of the page, and more so, to the God who inspired them. Allow God to lead you to a faith that leads to overcoming. May your faith grow and may that faith be a gift you claim and share.

—Russ Abel

THE MEASURE OF A MAN

The measure of a man is meticulously defined,
A tapestry crafted and skillfully designed.
Each action a layer that builds on the last,
Carefully constructing and weaving his past.

Conviction of spirit and honesty combine
Where integrity, truth, and honor entwine.
Compassion for others, not afraid to console
With passion and drive to stretch for the goal.

God's in the center of decisions he makes,
Seeking counsel for every direction he takes.
His principles strong, with no compromise:
No hidden agendas, masquerades, or disguise.

A firm guiding hand at the opportune time,
A shoulder to cry on, a poetic rhyme.
With loyalty and trust, ambition and pride,
He stands on his faith, committed to his bride.

The same around others as he is all alone,
He prospers in the Word as his soul has grown.
He courageously stands when most simply ran:
These are the qualities that measure a man.

Someday, up in heaven, I'm going to apply
For a job with angels in painting the sky.

A DEFINING MOMENT

A Sunday night gathering of community youth,
A chance to deliver and witness the truth.
Our group had drawn up some colorful signs
With motivational sayings and creative lines.

The noise level rose with a buzz in the air.
Many were surprised when he showed up there.
He walked with a swagger, the epitome of cool,
The basketball star from an arch-rival school.

My first impression was of an arrogant child,
A little too cocky and a little too wild.
As the kids settled in and gathered around,
A spelling mistake on a poster was found.

Some were poking fun in a damaging way.
"What idiot wrote that?" I heard someone say.
The unwitting culprit became easy to spot,
Sinking in her chair, hoping not to get caught.

The shy timid girl was now fighting back tears,
Facing devastation from ridiculing peers.
I observed it unfolding in tragic detail,
A public bashing was about to unveil.

I was considering how to put out this flame,
When *star-kid* stood up, accepting the blame.
He called it a test that would measure how long
It took them to notice which sign was done wrong.

They all had a laugh and got back on track.
The weight of the world lifted off of her back.
A defining moment where character shined,
A fragile young spirit was not undermined.

After the service, he was helping clean up.
I poured out some juice and offered a cup.
I stated, "You know people watch what you do.
Is breaking the commandments a habit for you?"

He was startled at first 'til I gave him a wink,
Stalling for a moment by sipping his drink.
He said, "I often am judged by what people see,
But I have a Savior who stands up for me!"

He stuck out his hand to give me a shake.
A gesture I thought very few kids would make.
"I apologize, sir, for crossing the line."
I said, "No, son, I'm sorry. The error was mine."

Stealing the glory that belongs to the Lord
May come at a price that you cannot afford.

If you don't learn to praise Him through serious blows,
Then who will you praise when success overflows?

When we honor our past, our future will last.

AMBITIOUSLY CONTENT

Can we be ambitious in seeking desires,
Yet still be content like the Bible requires?
Does saving one cause the other to be spent?
Can we possibly be "ambitiously content"?

Is it a trite contradiction to have some of each?
Should we strive for the goals it takes work to reach?
Are we way too ambitious or far too content?
Should we keep pushing forward or simply relent?

Does being content mean you don't have a dream?
Should we ever stop striving to build self-esteem?
Does showing ambition mean win at all costs?
Should we simply accept defeat when we've lost?

Embrace our ambition or nurture contentment,
What is the message that God's Word has sent?
Do we think that somehow God is confused?
Has this awkward dilemma left you amused?

Maybe *content* means to be satisfied
If we've given our best at whatever we've tried.
And maybe God wants us ambitious in ways,
That follow His calling and bring forth His praise.

So are you ambitious, or are you content?
If your answer is "Yes," we'll know what you meant.

A BURDEN OR A BLESSING?

We wonder why God would let things occur
That are certainly not the result we'd prefer.
With requirements too great to push on ahead,
We'd gladly endure almost anything instead.

We don't understand. How could this be true?
A roadblock to all that we've tried to pursue.
We question God's wisdom in anger and despair.
We might even wonder, "Does God really care?"

That's when we need Jesus to comfort our soul,
To fight through the challenge that's taken a toll.
If we pooled all our problems, then drew from a sack,
We'd likely discover we'd want our own back.

Perspectives can change with a new point of view,
When we follow our purpose, as God wants us to.
God's grace can transform what seems so oppressing;
This burden we bear, may well be a blessing.

We hear the commandments, but at times we assume
They may be suggestions with negotiating room.

Drink from the water that quenches your thirst.
Things will work out if you seek the Lord first.

EVER-AWARE

Are we *ever-aware* of the presence of God?
Do we take time to listen as angels applaud?
Can others see Christ come alive in our heart?
Are we using our faith to make demons depart?

Is it clear in our mind what path we should seek?
Do we call on the power of words that we speak?
Is He first in our life, or an occasional thought?
If Christ was illegal would we even get caught?

Do we put on the armor of God every day?
Has it been quite a while since we took time to pray?
Are the struggles of life distorting our view?
Does our passion convey what we know to be true?

It occurred to me God wasn't likely to say,
"It never occurred, I should do it your way."
In a world of distractions, distortions, and fraud,
Are we *ever-aware* of the presence of God?

It's not about what you believe God can do,
It's whether you believe He is talking to you.

Honorable words draw character lines;
Honoring your words is when character shines.

WITH ONE LAST BREATH

How will it go with your very last breath?
Have you really considered your ultimate death?
Will you know that it's coming with time to prepare?
Will it happen so quickly it's suddenly there?

Will scenes from your life flash in your eyes?
Will thoughts be consumed with what-ifs and whys?
Will you run to the light without doubt or fear?
Are you sure where you're going, will it be crystal clear?

Is your spirit convicted, salvation been won?
Will you capture the promise God made with His Son?
Will you find you decided just a little too late
Or celebrate life with those at the gate?

HEAVENLY WHITE-OUT

I dreamed that I went to heaven last night;
I followed a peaceful and comforting light.
Some friends were there who'd gone on before,
To tell me my future, what I had in store.

They carried a book, they said, about me.
They warned that it wouldn't be easy to see.
"All you have done has been written down here."
I opened it up with understandable fear.

"Your home is in heaven, you've accepted the Son.
Your deeds will determine the rewards you have won."
My mind was racing as I opened the book.
Discretions were flashing, I was scared just to look.

I scanned through some pages, but all I could find
Were good things I'd done. I sure didn't mind.
Elated at things that it seemed were omitted,
I couldn't find any of the sins I'd committed.

My friends were like kids in a free candy store,
Watching my reaction, they'd seen this before.
When they asked if I had any questions for now?
I didn't want to say something's missing somehow.

So I asked, "What are all the blank spaces I see?"
They all burst out laughing, the joke was on me.
They explained the book will record every task,
But God then forgives us whenever we ask.

Transgressions forgotten, the words are replaced
With heavenly white-out, your sins are erased.
When I woke that morning, things weren't the same.
I asked for forgiveness while praising His name.

JUST SOW THE SEEDS

We each have a job in God's grand design.
Just sow the seeds, they will grow in time.
It may only take a small piece of ground.
Just sow the seeds wherever you're bound.

You don't often see results that take place.
Just sow the seeds like a marathon race.
Someone will harvest them after they grow.
Just sow the seeds, no matter how slow.

God doesn't ask that we tend to the crop.
Just sow the seeds wherever they drop.

Some will grow, and others will not.
Just sow the seeds with all that you've got.

Some will grow fast but then fade away.
Just sow the seeds to someone today.
Some will be lost on ears that won't hear.
Just sow the seeds to anyone near.

Some will grow strong in character and soul.
Just sow the seeds—your ultimate goal.
Remember what God requires us to do:
Just sow the seeds that were given to you.

THE PERFECT GIFT

The difficult journey through store shelves you sift
To find that distinctive and just-perfect gift,
Something so special for someone somewhere,
The gift that will show how you really care.

But what can you do for that one on your list
With everything already, or so you insist.
You've exhausted the places you know to explore.
Maybe their gift shouldn't come from a store.

It could be a gift you creatively make,
Or maybe your gift is the time that you take,
Something inspired by the sweat of your brow,
Or some special skill you teach them somehow.

You could give a gift that will truly endure.
Their soul may be dying and you hold the cure.
God gave us a gift that He wants us to share,
So one day in heaven you both will be there.

197

He gave us His Son to die for our sins.
Accepting this gift is where life begins,
So maybe the most perfect gift you could give
Is to tell them the way to eternally live.

A JOYFUL NOISE

We get all fired up, we shout and scream.
As loud as we can, we cheer on our team.
Enthusiasm rules, excitement fills the air.
Next week we will barely recall being there.

A temporary high from seeds that won't grow,
Praising the actions of those we don't know.
What if we decided to do the same thing
When the praise team at church rises to sing?

If we shout, "Hallelujah!" at the top of our lungs,
If we cry out, "Praise God!" with angelic tongues,
If we raise up our hands like we scored on the play,
The Father might greet us the very same way.

Let's ruffle the shingles and make the walls shake.
Let's rattle the rafters with praises we make.
Let's wake herald angels, make them say, "Hark!"
Let's cause them to point down to this very mark.

Why don't we give out our thunderous applause
To our Father who loves us, despite all our flaws?
God's Word says to shout out our joyful rejoice.
He gave us free will, it's simply a choice.

So, don't move your lips with a lingering haze,
Come on and join in our exuberant praise!

Step up from your rut, step out from the crowd,
God wants us excited, triumphant, and loud!

BREAKFAST OF CHAMPIONS

Each day I wake up and shout, "Thank You, Lord!"
I put on my armor, my shield, and my sword.
I prepare in advance for the battle I face,
I remember the tears that I cannot erase.

I stop for a moment to listen and hear,
To make sure I know my direction is clear.
I go in my mind to kneel at the throne
With all my transgressions blatantly shown.

I ask for forgiveness from all that I've done;
I pledge once again my belief in the Son.
I nod my head, knowing my place is secure;
No matter what happens, I know this for sure.

I ask God to use me however He might,
Let me be the beacon, out casting His light.
I state my amens and open my eyes,
Ready for whatever the Enemy tries.

I gaze out to see what the angels have made:
A red ball of fire, bathed in orange marmalade.
I shake my head, knowing they've done it again,
What a glorious way for my day to begin.

ON A BIG BILLBOARD

I was driving home late on the highway one night,
My thoughts turned to how to make everything right.
I was so overwhelmed and struggling to find
A way out of being so completely behind.

The daily routine had taken its toll;
My schedule had somehow taken control.
I'd lost all my passion, my hope, and my drive.
The dreams I once had were just barely alive.

Asking for help was never my way,
But with little choice left, I decided to pray.
Then an answer appeared, it was surely divine.
God wrote it down on a big billboard sign.

It wasn't some brilliant marketing campaign.
It wasn't some catchy poetic refrain.
Just two simple words and the message was sent.
"I'm Available," it read, and I knew what it meant.

Would you answer your cell in the midst of a prayer,
If you believed the presence of God was there?

Is the abundance of fear to follow God's plan
Simply a lack of belief that He can?

I DON'T RECALL

I wonder what God was thinking when He made
Our brains in a way that our memories fade.
Like a computer, why can't our memories last?
Why can't we record and recall from the past?

Memories we never considered would leave
Are lost and forgotten, unable to retrieve.
A few still remain, refusing to fall,
The ones that we treasure and often recall.

Remember that very first look in their eyes?
That victory won after so many tries?
Right where you were on some magical day?
That diving catch made for the game-winning play?

The words to a song you've not heard in years?
That day someone special brought you to tears?
The highs become higher, the lows even lower,
Simple things seem to be coming back slower.

I've lost all the faces of friends who have gone.
I've had to let go. I've had to move on.
Some days I can hardly remember at all.
What point was I making? Oh yes, I recall…

If God hadn't made our brains to forget,
We might then get lost in a sea of regret.
When we focus on now, not what has been done,
We can focus on sharing the news of His Son.

Chapter 13: Authority (Spiritual Warfare)

Authority: Power, victory, triumphant, influence.

"For we do not wrestle against flesh and blood, but against principalities, against powers, against the rulers of the darkness of this age, against spiritual hosts of wickedness in the heavenly places" (Ephesians 6:12).

What to consider:

- We live in a spiritual world. There are forces that we often call on unknowingly. Are there times in your life when it was evident evil forces were against you?
- What does it mean to have "authority" over demonic spirits? How do your words play a role in the spiritual world?

Eric Sparks is Marla's older brother. He pastors The Church at Mountain Home in Mountain Home, Arkansas with his wife, Andrea. To put it mildly, Eric is not shy about his faith. Some might even say he is loud and boisterous. His passion for the Lord is undeniable. The church is growing at an incredible rate because of Eric's leadership and blessings from God. He is not afraid to speak the Word. He and his family were worship leaders at several churches before being called to pastor. Worship is truly an experience with Eric. May God richly bless their ministry.

You can visit him and his church at www.TheChurchatMH.com.

Guest Foreword by Pastor Eric Sparks

My wife, Andrea, and I have the honor and privilege of pastoring an amazing family of God's sons and daughters at a church simply called The Church at Mountain Home. My sister is Marla, and I had the blessing of joining her and Kevin together in marriage. Kevin wrote the vows that I use now in many of the weddings I perform. I watched as they joined their amazing families together before God. Kevin and Marla met under a God directive and have encountered, endured, conquered, and survived countless trials and tribulations in their lives, probably more than ninety percent of the couples I know or have counseled. Their faith has grown.

God also gave birth to their ministry, *Words Do Matter.* My sister has an amazing eye for photography, and Kevin has a unique ability in writing poetic parables. They understand and comprehend the importance of *words* and how to use them. "Death and life are in the power of the tongue, and those who love it will eat its fruit" (Proverbs 18:21). Just imagine, we have been given authority by the Lord Jesus Christ Himself, Creator of all things. "Behold, I give you the authority to trample on serpents and scorpions, and over all the power of the enemy, and nothing shall by any means hurt you" (Luke 10:19). Serpents and scorpions are biblical expressions for demons and evil spirits.

In Mark 11:23 Jesus tells us that we can move mountains that stand in our way if we: 1) *believe* without doubt in our hearts, and 2) *speak* the words we want. Why must we speak out the words? Because the Bible tells us that's how God's authority works. Words spoken with belief and authority do *not* return void. *Words really do matter.*

—Eric Sparks

A TROUBLED NATION

We can easily justify whatever we do.
Not knocking excuses; I've used a few too.
With lines being crossed between right and wrong,
Evil now resides where it does not belong.

Criminals are victims in the eyes of the court,
From lawyers with incentive to twist and contort.
Truth becomes second to political rant,
With media determined to mislead and slant.

The term *liability*, now forefront in mind,
Integrity and honor not common to find.
Lies labeled *normal*, as a part of the game.
Acts of destruction bring fortune and fame.

A country once strong where freedom rang proud,
Replaced by deception that screams out so loud.
I don't know the answers but if I would guess,
God won't continue putting up with this mess.

But still I have hope that never deters.
My faith will not falter, whatever occurs.
This crippling disease threatening our land
Will not change the fact that God's in command.

Someday I pray that our children will see
The only true way for us to be free.
The answer is simple, honest, and pure:
Our nation is troubled and Christ is the cure.

We live in a Spirit-filled world. Often we inadvertently invite spirits with the words we speak. When someone asks how you are, do you answer tired, busy, or stressed? Do you play the *"Who's busier?"* game with people? Our words are a creative force; are we personally inviting these trouble-causing spirits to wreak havoc in our lives? There is a better way—God's way. This poem is about spiritual warfare and the authority we have to change it. It is perhaps the most important story God has ever inspired me to write.

THE PARTY'S OVER

I fell to my knees from feeling so weak,
"Somebody help me," was all I could speak.
Right when I thought I had figured things out,
Fear sauntered in and introduced *Doubt*.
The twins came over, *Dismay* and *Despair*;
Then *Apathy* appeared: "Does anyone care?"

Disgust and *Disdain* knocked on my door.
Disillusionment laughed at what was in store.
Envy and *Pride* cried unanimous cheers;
Doom and *Desperation* were invoking fears.
Defiance brought a sign, "Come watch him fall."
A gruesome, grotesque masquerade ball.

The party complete full of *demons* and *ghouls,*
A chaotic nightmare, void of all rules.
I ventured outside away from the noise,
Despondent by actions that *Evil* employs.
I sat on the porch, hands over my face,
The stench of *Destruction* dispensing *Disgrace*.

I cried out, "Dear Lord, what more can I do?"
I jumped when a voice said, "It's all up to you."
I gathered my senses and offered a seat
To an elderly woman who lived down the street.
"That's quite a party you seem to be throwing."
I nodded my head, "It just keeps on growing."

She leaned in and whispered, "They run in packs,
Carefully planning these full-scale attacks."
I asked her the reason they all showed up here.
She said, "You empowered the illusion of *Fear*.
Without you to help them, their power is weak.
They gather up strength from words that you speak.

What you don't understand, regardless it's true:
God gave authority over *spirits* to *you*."
Something made sense in what she had said.
She changed the perception I had in my head.
So I stormed in the house with *Courage* and *Peace*,
Screaming, "It's over! This party must cease!"

Conviction paraded as *Faith* filled my heart;
In the name of Jesus, I demanded they part!
Their revelry turned to howling and shrieks:
A bellowing *Angst* echoed out from the peaks.
They whined and moaned, but followed command.
Hope cleansed the room and *Truth* took a stand.

My newfound friend was no longer there.
I shouted out, "Thank you!" into the night air.
Hearing commotion, "For what?" asked my wife.
"That church-lady friend of yours just saved my life."
"Grace?" she questioned. "Didn't you know?
Grace went to heaven almost two weeks ago."

"The Party's Over" contains one of the greatest biblical truths we can grasp. Often we have created our own situation with words we have spoken. God gave us authority over spirits in the name of Jesus. Can you imagine what that means? Authority is a word we often underestimate. Authority means the spirits must obey our commands in the name of Jesus if we believe. Wow, I guess we better be careful what we are commanding. The most significant thing we can create with our words is our eternal salvation. With words, we claim our place in heaven, or we claim a different eternity by a lack of words. Don't wait. Satan's biggest deception is not that Jesus isn't real, but that you have plenty of time to decide.

Fear is a sword that Satan will swing.
Courage is the shield that faith will bring.

UNMASKING UNTRUTH

"It's never too late," a friend of mine said.
"Oh, but it is," I replied, "if you're dead."
There's plenty of time, the message implied.
But what if it's gone before you decide?

"You see," I explained, "it's a spiritual war."
The strategic deception is to keep giving more.
More and more things that will busy our lives.
Distracting our focus so we won't realize.

If Satan can wage a *too-busy* assault,
The outcome will be—he wins by default.
The decision we have that determines our fate,
Once time has run out, will then be too late!

MARKETING DECEPTION

It starts with a goal, the truth to conceal.
Confusing the facts from that which is real.
A strategy they seem to consistently use
To continually state their contention as news.

Come up with a thought, completely absurd,
Treat it as though it's a fact that's occurred.
Persistently repeat it, as if it were known,
And a few will believe the seeds that are sown.

A few becomes some, some leads to more.
Soon many will claim to have "heard that before."
There's no need for evidence supporting their claim,
They'll quote a *quote* expert, recognizable name.

In time then, the thought, with no basis in fact,
Becomes *commonly known*, roots deep intact.
A deceptive illusion, accepted by those
Unaware, uninformed, how the strategy goes.

"There's no room left," you may have been told.
"Just a broken-down stable to shelter the cold."
When we've nowhere to go and our path is unsure,
If we trust in the Lord, great miracles occur.

DECEPTION REVEALED

The art of destruction, with danger concealed
Strategically, purposefully, left unrevealed.
Cloaked and disguised as something it's not,
Lurking in shadows of lies we have bought.

Deceptive, deliberate attempts to deceive,
Stirring confusion in what we believe.
Courageous and bold, intentional and keen,
Masquerading as good, honest, and clean.

It's a spiritual war, the ammunition is fear;
Things are not always the way they appear.
There are forces around us with one common goal:
Hiding the truth from our eternal soul.

ILLOGICAL LOGIC

I once had a friend, the logical kind.
He based his beliefs on facts he could find.
When it came to the Bible, he couldn't conceive
How a logical mind could possibly believe.

"It's too far-fetched to really be true,
A completely unlikely improbable view.
If God existed, then He would reveal
Himself here on earth to prove He was real."

I responded, just a little confused,
"That's exactly the method He already used."

DETENTION INTERVENTION

I unjustly relinquished my Saturday morning,
A detention received with no prior warning.
No chance to reply, no evidence to defend,
When I casually mentioned the church I attend.

The kid next to me looked Gothic in black,
Stoned out of his mind, all messed up on crack.
A satanic tattoo was etched down his arm.
An upside-down cross he wore like a charm.

He carried a book full of witchcraft and such.
The teacher looked through it but didn't say much.
With a cocky defiance and rebellious trance,
It seemed like a challenge, so I took a chance.

I asked what it was they had gotten him for.
He said, "Spitting gum on the coach's clean floor."
"That's it?" I cried out. "It wasn't those chains,
The guns, or the knives, or running with gangs?"

He said, "They're afraid of taking control.
There are too many of us for them to patrol."
I said, "Can I ask what you're trying to convey?
Are you sending a message by dressing that way?"

He stuck out his chin and replied, rather proud,
"I won't be considered a part of the crowd.
I want to be different. I want to stand out.
Authority can't define what it is I'm about."

"You want to stand out?" I said. "Sorry, that's lame.
Have you not even noticed you all look the same?
Apparently I've discovered a much better way.
If you want to rebel, you should learn how to pray."

He thought for a moment, then said "I agree.
You're simply demanding your right to be free."
So I opened my Bible to John 3:16,
"If you'll read this and pray, you'll see what I mean."

That's when the teacher found reason to speak.
"That's it! You two are back here next week.
You know the rules, I can't let that occur."
The kid rolled his eyes, then spouted, "But sir…

You mean I'm in trouble for saying a prayer,
But if I do drugs, you don't really care?
I can speak about evil or some satanic game,
But I can't even mention the Bible by name?"

The teacher responded, "I don't make the rules."
The kid looked at me, and said, "Rules by fools."
As we walked out the door, he said, "This is cool.
They've no right to keep us from praying in school."

He stopped at the trash, tossed in his book.
"Can I borrow your Bible, maybe give it a look?"
"It's yours," I responded by tipping my hat.
"I'll see you next week, who knows after that."

THE LIST

Something was wrong, I had to insist,
Explaining to them why I should be on the list.
A bookkeeping error has somehow occurred,
For I am a Christian, or haven't you heard?

My place is reserved, I know this because
I've carefully studied what a good Christian does.
I've carried my Bible on public display.
I've strung fancy words when it came time to pray.

At appropriate times I've lifted my hands.
I listened to music from pop Christian bands.
I knew all the lyrics of songs we would sing.
I've boasted how church is a "wonderful thing."

I took all the steps a Christian would take.
I made all the moves a Christian might make.
I spoke out the words, professing to be
A Christian believer to all who would see.

During the sermons, I even took notes.
At times I would reference some biblical quotes.
I was an elder, a teacher, a consummate friend.
I learned all the proper responses to send.

After asking again to take one more look,
They explained to me why I was not in the book;
For had I known Jesus, that would have sufficed,
But I was a Christian who didn't know Christ.

FRIEND OR ACQUAINTANCE?

On the day you meet Jesus, how will it go?
Will He run to embrace you, or come up real slow?
Will He throw out His arms like a best friend would,
Or just shake your hand like a businessman should?

Will He welcome you home, call you by name,
Or give you a look like you-all-look-the-same?
Will He talk to your soul since He knows who you are,
Or stay on the surface like a friend from afar?

Will He smile saying, "Come, I've prepared a place,"
Or leave you alone to find your own space?
If He treats you the way He was treated by you,
Would He treat you as someone whom He never knew?

On the day you meet Jesus, how will it go?
Will you run to embrace Him, or saunter in slow?
Will you open your arms as wide as can be,
Or asking forgiveness, fall down on one knee?

Will you open your eyes to look at His face,
Or humbly cower in fear of disgrace?
Will you show Him respect, which is certainly due
For someone who gave up their life just for you?

Will you act like a salesman, constructing a deal,
Or know in your heart the friendship was real?
Will you stand with assurance, faithful and strong,
As He welcomes you home to where you belong?

A TALE OF TWO KINGS

There once was a king, proper and proud,
Who lived in a castle overlooking the crowd.
He made up commandments for all to obey.
His picture was posted on public display.

He commanded his army with a decorative sword.
"His people," he called them, addressed him as Lord.
He taxed all the wages they worked so hard for,
Then basked in the glory of "helping the poor."

He thought people loved him; what he did not know,
The respect he was given was only for show.
There once was a King, unlike all the rest,
Who wasn't concerned about who might be the best.

He taught how to serve, how to put others first.
He spoke about water that quenches one's thirst.
He comforted those with burdensome loads;
He stayed by their side down treacherous roads.

He loved them so much, He was willing to be
Crucified on a cross so they could be free.
Forgiveness of sin, despite what they'd done,
There once was a King who was God's precious Son.

"God Wrote It Down" is a true story. It was tricky because this couple was so excited about their "revelation" that a loving God couldn't send anyone to hell. It just wasn't biblical. I don't know if I helped or confused, but they heard the truth.

GOD WROTE IT DOWN

I listened intently to what they had said,
Knowing that they had been somehow misled.
The challenge I faced was how to dispel
The notion that, "No one was going to hell."

After all, they determined in a sensible way,
"A loving God never could send us away."
Do I tell them they're wrong, explain to them why,
Or simply say nothing and not even try?

If I choose to react, will they think I'm rude?
Am I risking a holier-than-thou attitude?
If I keep my silence, will they think I agree?
I wonder what Jesus would do, were He me?

I asked myself what kind of risk I should take,
Knowing full well that their souls were at stake.
I said, being mindful of their point of view,
"I know how you feel. I've felt that way too."

"It's hard to envision God turning away
Any of His children come judgment day.
What I've found is this: He gave us the right
To flee to the darkness or to run toward the light."

"The fact that God loves us is logically why
He grants us the freedom to live or to die.
He even wrote it down, so we won't have to guess.
Heaven is chosen through words we confess."

GOD'S CALLING

I was still a bit groggy when I answered the phone.
I couldn't quite read the name that was shown.
"Hello," I stammered in my gravelly voice.
"Wake up!" I heard. "Prepare to rejoice!"
"What? Who is this?" I started to say,
Already thinking this must go away.

"Can you hold for God?" came over the line.
I paused just to think, then said, "Okay, fine."
I knew it was some kind of marketing call,
Convinced that I finally had now heard it all.
As I sat there on hold, the question I had—
Should I hang up on God or would that be bad?

"Yeah, right," I reasoned, "God's calling me?"
So I looked on my phone for the caller ID.
As if someone somehow inserted a name,
"God" was there scrolling my screen like a game.
As I put the receiver back up to my ear,
If just for a second, I trembled in fear.

The music had stopped for a moment or two,
Enough that I spoke the words, "God, is that You?"
I admit to the fact that, despite unbelief,
When the dial tone began, I felt some relief.
If it truly was God, I thought, what would He say?
Maybe, "I'm calling since you rarely pray."

I'd gotten too involved in my daily routine.
God became something I squeezed in between.
It seemed so ironic, with so much at stake,
The difference that one simple phone call could make.

Chapter 14: Belief (Salvation)

Belief: Faith, assurance, hope, salvation, eternal life.

"For God so loved the world, that He gave His only begotten Son, that whoever believes in Him should not perish but have everlasting life" (John 3:16).

What to consider:

- Are you sure of your eternal salvation?
- Do you have a personal relationship with Jesus?
- Do you really believe, or just hope what He says is true?

Adam Detamore is our lead pastor at the church we attend, Realife Church in Greenfield, Indiana. Adam's enthusiasm and passion to serve the Lord is contagious. The Lord has blessed him and his wife, Kristin, with a divine calling to reach people for Jesus Christ. Their mission statement is "Creating an experience people love so they can experience the love of Christ." You can visit them at: www. realifechurch.org.

Guest Foreword by Pastor Adam Detamore

They say, "Sound waves never die, they simply go on." If that's true, our words literally have eternal implications. As a husband, father, and pastor of a steadily growing church for the past ten years, I have seen the power of our words. Whether they are words of love or correction to a child, words of encouragement or criticism to an employee or coworker, or words of affection or anger toward a spouse, *words do matter*. However, I would argue that it isn't the words themselves that are powerful. It is the *belief* in those words that empowers them. It's when we believe our father when he tells us how strong we are that our chest puffs up. It's when we believe our spouse when she says "I love you" that our heart goes pitter-patter. We begin to live when we believe the words of Jesus: "I have come that they may have life, and that they may have it more abundantly" (John 10:10). While you cannot control the words that are said about you, you can control what you believe about those words.

As I have watched Kevin Pace the last several years, I have seen the power of belief in action. Doctors, as well as others, have told Kevin what he will or will not be able to do. Kevin has chosen to believe God's Word: "I can do all things through Christ who strengthens me" (Philippians 4:13). "With God all things are possible" (Matthew 19:26). "For I know the thoughts that I think toward you, says the Lord, thoughts of peace and not of evil, to give you a future and a hope" (Jeremiah 29:11). As you read this book, I pray you are encouraged by Kevin's belief.

—Adam Detamore

220

COURT DATE

"How do you plead?" he shouted and stared.
I was startled and dazed, alone, cold, and scared.
My mind was confused and starting to race.
What are these charges I now seem to face?

Last thing I remembered was hitting my head.
Maybe that's it, I thought, maybe I'm dead.
It was difficult to orient myself to the room,
Giving off an impending dark feeling of doom.

A husky voice bellowed, "Do you have a plea?"
I didn't understand what was happening to me.
"It's a simple little question. I'll ask once again.
In the life you were given, were you guilty of sin?"

I was seeking composure, unsure what to do.
I stammered confessing, "There have been a few."
He began to unravel a lengthy white scroll.
As he scanned down the pages, I saw his eyes roll.

I wanted to speak, not knowing if I should.
Then, "Guilty as charged!" as gavel struck wood.
"But wait," I objected, "that doesn't make sense.
Have I no opportunity to mount a defense?"

"I have made mistakes like your document reads,
But I've given my time, done many good deeds."
He gave me a nod, but proclaimed, "It's too late!
The presence of sin cannot pass through the gate."

"The works you have done are not up for review.
Our directive is simple: who gets to go through."
"Your sentence is death," he proceeded to say.
"How will you resolve this debt you must pay?"

I felt my knees buckle as I dropped to the floor.
A light started glowing like I've not seen before.
A resounding voice echoed and began to cascade,
"By the blood of the Lamb, his debt has been paid!"

"For he hath proclaimed his faith in the Son,
As written in the Word, now let it be done."
That gavel slammed down, an ear-popping sound:
"In light of the evidence that now has been found,

With debts all paid up and a life free of sin,
Well done, faithful servant, you may now enter in."
As a door opened up, light shone on my bed.
My wife said, "Wake up! I know you're not dead."

"Court Date" was completely a gift of the Holy Spirit. It started with the first line, and the rhyme dictated the story. I was as surprised where the story went as if I was reading the story for the first time.

When time becomes short and death becomes real,
We clearly embrace the way that we feel.
We stop to consider what matters the most:
The Father, the Son, and the Holy Ghost.

WHO'S TO BLAME?

On the first few holes, on a couple of shots,
His clubs took the wrath of his frustrated thoughts.
A few salty words on a high scoring round,
A tendency to blame anything to be found.

When I casually asked him what church he attends,
His attitude changed, attempting amends.
He explained how he used to go "all of the time,"
But his pastor had committed a very bad crime.

When he told me he vowed not to go back again,
"Imagine," I reasoned, "a church full of sin!"
As if in agreement, he nodded his head,
Missing the sarcasm in what I had said.

"If I could, let me ask," I went on to say,
"It's been a few holes, I've seen how you play.
Those clubs that you carry seem innocent enough,
Yet still take the blame for shots that you duff.

The stance that you're taking, while seemingly strong,
Has *you* paying the price for somebody's wrong.
Will that be your answer at eternity's gate,
When asked why you've chosen such a fiery fate?"

"Who's to Blame?" is based on a true experience. I played golf with a guy, and this really was his excuse for why he would miss out on heaven's rewards. Being willing to go to hell for someone else's sin— that's either extremely courageous or eternally dumb! Do you have an excuse? Any one will do.

TOO LITTLE, TOO LATE

If you run from a challenge when things become rough,
And think to yourself, ***That'll be good enough***,
You'll likely discover when dreams start to fall
The extra for excellence is deceptively small.

If you constantly look for corners to cut,
And ***why*** explanations include the word ***but,***
The harvest you hoped for from seeds you have sown
May not have had all they need to have grown.

If your goal is discovering the least you must do,
And that minimum effort seems plenty to you,
The thing you may hear as you stand at the gate,
"Depart from Me, sinner: too little, too late."

GO MAKE DISCIPLES

Darkness can never overshadow the light.
Authority is yours in the spiritual fight.

Go change the world by letting yours shine.
Your duty is simple; your calling, divine.

Go make disciples throughout this great land.
Tell them of Jesus by taking a stand.

CHRISTIAN SAYINGS

Salvation is not a goal you achieve,
But rather a gift, which by grace you receive.

God's grace can transform what seems so oppressing;
This burden we bear may well be a blessing.

The seeds have been sown, the crop has been tilled.
The harvest is ready, God's promise fulfilled.

It's hard to imagine, it's tough to conceive
How anyone watching could still not believe.

When we speak about faith, why is it we feel
We must know it all, to make it sound real?

As the breathtaking beauty of God becomes clear,
You'll walk through the valley, absent of fear.
Nothing can shake you when faith intercedes;
God's precious grace will fill all your needs.

The sun will rise. The sun will fall.
The Son who fell rose for us all.

If God makes a proud and magnificent tree,
From a tiny little seed that's determined to be,
What would He do if He were to see
That passion, desire, and conviction in me?

I prayed for God's blessing, but rather I found
If I'd be a blessing, then mine would come 'round.

If you seek sanctuary, your journey is done;
Peace can be found in the arms of the Son.

The harvest you reap when the crops have all grown
Will be the result of the seeds you have sown.

We cast out the line, we reel in the bait.
We witness the truth and then patiently wait.
Some will ignore us, some will just glance,
For many we could be their very last chance.

A child in a manger, the story begins:
A Savior is born to die for our sins.
The gift of our Father's magnificent grace,
That ensures for us all an eternal place.

There are bridges we cross on the path that we seek.
There are bridges we build with words that we speak.
If we speak out the words and seek to be filled,
A path to the cross is the bridge that we build.

The best words you'll ever be privileged to hear,
The words of the Father, you will always hold dear.
"You've followed My Word and accepted My Son.
My good faithful servant, I tell you, well done!"

The same way the sun dances light through the trees,
When the Son shines in you, it's what everyone sees.

We'll "tell the whole world" of God's Holy Word,
When it could be our neighbor who never has heard.

The sun will bring life to the seeds that you've laid.
The Son will give life, for your debt has been paid.

When I learned that success wasn't all up to me,
When I gave it to God unconditionally,
When I learned any glory was not rightly mine,
Only then did the light of the world start to shine.

With so little time to do what needs done,
When it seems we're behind before we've begun,
The best thing to do at the start of each day,
Is ask God to help us and take time to pray.

In the journey of life, there's one lesson I've learned:
Do not try to straighten a road that God's turned.

If God gave the spider the ability to weave
An artistic masterpiece, so hard to believe,
Why would we think God would choose
To deny us a talent that we could so use?

When storm clouds form and danger appears,
The shield of salvation will comfort your fears.

Is He first in our life, or an occasional thought?
If Christ was illegal, would we even get caught?

If you step out on faith, eyes fixed on the Son,
You might walk on water like Peter had done.

At times we're too focused on getting things done,
When all will work out if we just praise the Son.

As we stand at the gate that opens for few,
The blood on the cross will let us cross through.

Be wary of weary in doing good things,
For great are rewards that faithfulness brings.

WHERE DO YOU STAND?

One day each of us will have to answer the question, "Who was this man they call Jesus?" There is more historical evidence that He existed than for anyone in history. So the question is not did He exist, but rather who was He? Many will claim He was a great teacher or prophet. That is clearly true from the many things He was credited for saying. The issue is, He also claimed to be God. Was He a liar, spouting out gems of wisdom but all the while plotting a spectacular story that He knew wasn't true? Was He crazy, believing what couldn't possibly be true? Or was He who He said He was—our Lord in the flesh? These are the only three choices we have.

Does it seem plausible that eleven men scattered in all directions, scared for their lives, would band together to concoct a resurrection story that none would ever recant, even to their death? People are willing to die for a lot of things, but not to perpetuate a lie. Does it seem plausible that His tomb was empty when many with the incentive to stop the uprising could have easily found the body had it been stolen? Does it seem plausible that a mother could sit in silence and watch her son be crucified for something she knew was a lie? Would she not say, "He's crazy; punish him if you must, but don't kill him"?

It's interesting. With all the religions in the world, all but one of them asks or tells us what we must do to gain favor with its particular god. Only one is about what God has done for you. For it is by *grace* that we are allowed to enter eternity with God the Father. None of us deserves it, lest we should boast. Our relationship with God is rooted in our belief in Him and the fact that He sent His Son to die on the cross for the forgiveness of sins.

Doesn't science contradict the claims of the Bible? Anyone can say anything and if they say it enough it gains popularity. Doesn't the big bang theory conflict with the creation story? Scientists base this on calculations that the earth is much older than the Bible claims. However, there are lots of questions about their ideas to consider: Had they run their test on day one after creation, how old would the result say the earth was? Likely not one day. What about evolution? The truth is that evolution of particular species does exist. Humans have evolved and adapted, monkeys have evolved and adapted. However, there is no evidence that one species has ever become another. If monkeys evolved into humans, why are there still monkeys? Can't scientists show how life began? If you took all the greatest scientists in the history of the world and put them together saying, "Go ahead, create life," they could not produce one blade of grass without starting with a seed. The seed of life remains in the Creator's hands.

I am appealing to your sense of logic right now, but rarely does logic move anyone to make a decision. Satan's biggest lie is not that Jesus doesn't exist, it's that you have plenty of time to decide. Tomorrow is never promised. My hope and prayer is that these thoughts lead you to a decision about who Jesus was and is. Of course, it doesn't end there; even Satan believes in Jesus. Jesus wants you to come to Him. What you can find in giving your life to Jesus is a life-changing peace. You can have a personal relationship with the Maker of all things. Not that He will solve all your problems, but He will give you the strength and the understanding to face them.

I will end with my favorite story based on a true experience I had at a high school youth retreat. It is a powerfully simple prayer to use for any situation.

THE PERFECT PRAYER

I was leading the service at church Sunday night.
We were deep in the throes of a spiritual fight.
The preacher was gone, emotions ran high.
My first thought was no, but I knew I must try.
When it came time to pray, I wasn't prepared.
I was feeling the pressure as everyone stared.

In searching my mind for guiding direction,
My wandering eyes made an easy connection.
He was a principled man who never said much;
Most knew him for his compassionate touch.
Before I could weigh all the risks it involved,
I had asked him to pray—my problem was solved.

He reluctantly agreed with a nervous little smile,
Then started in, "God…" and paused for a while.
He struggled intently for words to compose.
As each moment passed, the room-tension rose.
A silent prayer, not what I first had in mind,
But we all had one going for words he could find.

A long awkward silence, I'd counted to ten,
When he finally yelled, "Help!" then a quiet, "amen."
Laughter burst out over what had occurred.
He captured our anguish with one masterful word.
This Spirit-filled man I had put on the spot,
Patiently waited for the answer he sought.

Our healing began from that heartfelt plea.
When we give it to God, He knows just what we need.
With hope now replacing any thoughts of despair,
I thanked him for praying the "perfect prayer."

Afterword

Life is full of extreme battles, ultimate tests, and terrifying tribulations. These trials will make us stronger if we persevere. Our greatest weapons during these times of struggle are the words we choose to speak. You put on the armor of God with your words. It is our choice to speak victory or speak defeat. Oftentimes, you will find you get exactly what you speak. If you answer *tired*, *busy*, or *stressed* to the simple question, "How are you?" guess what? That is exactly how you are. You've spoken it into existence. In this book, we have gone over fourteen power words that will help arm you for warfare. The power of the tongue should not be underestimated. You have that power when you believe.

- **Revelation** – First you have to realize you are in a fight.
- **Love** – Above all things, love one another.
- **Motivation** – Don't weary in well-doing, draw strength.
- **Passion** – Draw people around you with your desire.
- **Creativity** – You are a unique and magnificent creation.
- **Inspiration** – Always be open to, and look for, new ideas.
- **Leadership** – Others will follow if you choose to lead.
- **Servanthood** – He who is willing to be last will be first.
- **Character** – Don't let your battle define you.
- **Hope** – Don't ever lose it, or let anyone steal it.
- **Wisdom** – Your answer is often only one prayer away.
- **Faith** – Genuine childlike faith is the key to heaven.
- **Authority** – Be aware of spiritual warfare. Take control.
- **Belief** – You can have a relationship with Jesus Christ.

The Beginning – Go write your story. Always remember, Words Do Matter!

About the Author

Kevin writes the words, Marla snaps the photographs. Together they create incredible images that they sell as ready-to-frame, photographic, wedding-quality, linen-textured prints. Included is an acid-free backing board, a protective plastic seal, and an insert, telling the location of the photograph. Prints come in three basic sizes: 5x7, 8x10, and 11x14. Custom work and custom sizes are also available.

We would like to thank 5 Fold Media and especially Andy and Cathy Sanders for believing in this project.

Watch for other books coming soon from Words Do Matter!

Words Do Matter has over 200 original photo images with selected sayings from this book for sale on the website:

www.WordsDoMatter.com

To Contact Kevin & Marla Pace:

contact@wordsdomatter.com
kkpace@yahoo.com
marlapace@yahoo.com
www.wordsdomatter.com
Twitter: @wordsdomatter
Facebook: wordsdomatterart
317-724-9702

Ways of sharing *Words Do Matter.*

- First and foremost, pray for this ministry. Please pray specifically that God uses the material to touch people in just the right way.
- Share a copy with your pastor, youth group leader, small group study leader, or church library. Consider *Words Do Matter* in your next small group study selection process. Make it a church-wide initiative.
- Give copies to your friends, identifying the story/stories you would like them to read.
- Give copies as wedding, birthday, or housewarming gifts.
- Share with your friends on social media. Join in the online discussions. Give feedback. Promote, promote, promote!
- Consider using the book as a fundraiser for not-for-profits.
- Comment about a particular story or poem on our Facebook page.
- Use as clients' gifts, coaches' gifts, or as a rewards program.
- Drop off copies in waiting rooms you frequent. Have extra copies on hand for just the right moment that someone needs one of these stories. We have volume discounted pricing.
- Create a family discussion group as you share stories together at the dinner table.
- Read to your children, display to them that *Words Do Matter*.

Notes:

Made in the USA
Monee, IL
02 September 2019